Early Literacy Instruction for the New Millennium

Early Literacy Instruction

for the

New Millennium

edited by

W. Dorsey Hammond
Oakland University

Taffy E. Raphael
Center for the Improvement of Early Reading Achievement
Oakland University

Michigan Reading Association
Grand Rapids, Michigan

Center for the Improvement of Early Reading Achievement
Ann Arbor, Michigan

Michigan Reading Association
5241 Plainfield NE, Suite I
Box 10
Grand Rapids, Michigan 49525-1060

Center for the Improvement of Early Reading Achievement
University of Michigan
610 East University Avenue, Room 1600 SEB
Ann Arbor, Michigan 48109-1259

DESIGNED AND PRODUCED BY MODE DESIGN.

ISBN 0-9668496-1-2

Manufactured in the United States of America.

10 9 8 7 6 5 4 3 2 1

Contents

1   **Toward a More Complex View of Balance in the Literacy Curriculum** ·1
P. David Pearson, CIERA/Michigan State University
Taffy E. Raphael, CIERA/Oakland University

2   **Every Child a Reader: At Work in a First-Grade Classroom** ·23
Elfrieda H. Hiebert, CIERA/University of Michigan

3   **Diversity in a Democratic Society: Implications for Literacy Instruction** ·49
Barbara J. Diamond, Eastern Michigan University

4   **School-Family Connections: Why Are They So Difficult to Create?** ·73
Patricia A. Edwards, CIERA/Michigan State University

5   **A Michigan Early Literacy Parent/Teacher Collaboration** ·91
Deanna Birdyshaw, Michigan Department of Education

6   **A Balanced Early Literacy Curriculum: An Ecological Perspective** ·113
W. Dorsey Hammond, Oakland University

Preface

This book represents the joint effort of six Michigan literacy educators committed to the improvement of literacy skills for the young citizens of our state. Our goal was to provide teachers, administrators, and parents with a useful information source that summarizes current knowledge related to early literacy instruction. We thought it would be timely and helpful, given the often confusing and contradictory advice that has appeared in newspapers, magazines, and research journals in the past decade.

As contributing author Deanna Birdyshaw describes in her chapter, Michigan has a long history of close working relationships among the literacy educators in the State Department of Education, literacy teacher educators at our many state universities and colleges, the Michigan Reading Association (MRA), and local school personnel. Recently, we have added the Center for the Improvement of Early Reading Achievement (CIERA)—funded through a grant from the U.S. Department of Education—to the people and agencies within our state that are focusing on improving early reading instruction. This close collaboration is reflected in the representation of these various agencies whose members contributed the chapters that compose this book.

This book is designed to address major areas that support effective literacy education for the young learners within our state. The first chapter, by P. David Pearson of CIERA/Michigan State University and Taffy E. Raphael of CIERA/Oakland University, explains the concept of balance as it applies to the instructional programs that support literacy development for our students. The second chapter, by Elfrieda H. Hiebert of CIERA/University of Michigan, takes us into an exemplary first grade classroom where the principles for effective reading instruction identified by CIERA researchers are instantiated. The third chapter, by Barbara J. Diamond of Eastern Michigan University, focuses on the diverse learners who make up our classrooms. In the fourth chapter, Patricia A. Edwards of CIERA/Michigan State University highlights specific principles and programs for creating the strong home-school relationships so crucial to children's literacy learning. In the fifth chapter, Deanna Birdyshaw of the Michigan Department of Education traces the development of Michigan's Early Literacy Committee, an important collaboration among teachers, parents, teacher educators, and the State Department of Education for furthering effective instruction across our state. In the sixth and final chapter, W. Dorsey Hammond of Oakland University describes effective reading and writing instruction from his perspective as a teacher educator and teacher for more than 30 years.

We believe this book will be a useful tool for administrators interested in developing an exemplary early literacy program that reflects the best of curricular practices, for parents interested in developing a broad understanding of the issues that educators consider in creating strong literacy curricula, for teachers interested in enhancing their current practice, and for those in other states who are interested in the benefits of developing strong relationships among those interested in the education of young children.

We have many people to thank in bringing this project to fruition. We thank both the MRA and CIERA for their support of this project. Within these groups, we wish to note special recognition to Sue Szczeparski and her publications committee, Leonie Rose who serves as MRA's president, and MRA's Executive Director, Karen Katz. We thank Laurie Clark

Klavins at CIERA for her tireless efforts in editing the manuscript, and Tiff Crutchfield for his design. We thank the authors who contributed to this book for their hard work to develop their chapters under very tight deadlines. All are very busy and we appreciated their willingness to support this effort within our state. To Kathy Au, member of the Board of Directors of the International Reading Association, we thank you for your time and energy in creating the introduction to this book and setting our work within the national context. And last but not least, we thank both Joan Buffone and Jim Gavelek for their ongoing conversations about literacy theory and practice, and their support of our work.

We hope that our readers will find this book on literacy issues to be thoughtful, sometimes provocative, and hopefully helpful in your respective roles as educators, parents, and interested citizens. We share the goal of strengthening literacy programs across our state to help Michigan maintain its well-earned reputation for excellence in literacy education.

WDH & TER
March, 1999

Contributors

Kathryn H. Au, Professor in the College of Education at the University of Hawaii at Manoa, has previously worked as a researcher, curriculum developer, teacher educator, and classroom teacher. Her research interest is the school literacy development of students of diverse cultural and linguistic backgrounds. She has published over sixty professional articles. She is president of the National Reading Conference and of the Aloha State Council of the International Reading Association, and has served as a vice-president of the American Educational Research Association (AERA). She was recognized as a Distinguished Scholar by the AERA Standing Committee on the Role and Status of Minorities in Educational Research and was named a fellow of the National Conference on Research in Language and Literacy.

Deanna Birdyshaw is currently a supervisor of Reading for the Michigan Department of Education. A former secondary English teacher, she is completing her doctoral work in Literacy at Oakland University. For the last three years, Deanna has organized and directed the Michigan Early Literacy Committee while continuing to establish close working relationships with individuals and institutions in Michigan committed to the improvement of literacy practices. She is a frequent presenter at state and national literacy conferences.

Barbara J. Diamond is currently a Professor of Education at Eastern Michigan University where she teaches courses in multicultural literacy and reading and writing methods in urban settings. She is co-author of *Multicultural Literacy: Mirroring the Reality of the Classroom* (Longman), which chronicles her research and collaborative work with public schools.

Patricia A. Edwards is a Professor in the College of Education at Michigan State University and a Principal Investigator of the national Center for the Improvement of Early Reading Achievement (CIERA). She is currently on the Board of Directors of the International Reading Association. Professor Edwards is widely published and a recognized national authority on family literacy and role of parents in the learning-to-read-and-write process.

W. Dorsey Hammond is a Professor of Reading at Oakland University. He is a recipient of the Oakland University Excellence in Teaching Award and a Distinguished Professorship awarded by Michigan Governing Boards of Universities. Professor Hammond's interests are in the comprehensive process and issue of emergent literacy. He is a frequent presenter at state, national, and international meetings on issues of literacy.

Elfrieda H. Hiebert is the Director of the Center for the Improvement of Early Reading Achievement (CIERA) and a Professor in the School of Education at the University of Michigan. Professor Hiebert has worked in the field of early reading acquisition for more than twenty-five years, first as a teacher of primary-level students in central California and subsequently as a teacher educator and researcher at the Universities of Kentucky, Colorado-Boulder, and Michigan. Professor Hiebert's research on how instruction and assessment practices influence literacy acquisition, especially among low-income children, has been widely published and cited.

P. David Pearson holds the John A. Hannah Distinguished Professorship of Education in the College of

Education at Michigan State University, where he is a member of the Department of Teacher Education and Department of Counseling, Educational Psychology, and Special Education. As a research scientist and Co-Director of the Center for the Improvement of Early Reading Achievement (CIERA), he continues to pursue a line of research related to reading instruction and reading assessment policies and practices at local, state, and national levels.

Taffy E. Raphael is a Professor in the Department of Reading and Language Arts at Oakland University where she teaches courses in literature-based reading instruction. She has conducted research on strategy instruction in reading and writing, children's and teachers' classroom talk about text, and teacher inquiry. Her research has been published in journals such as *The Reading Teacher*, *Language Arts* and *Reading Research Quarterly*. She has co-authored *Creating an Integrated Approach to Literacy Instruction* and *Early Literacy Instruction* with Elfrieda H. Hiebert, co-edited *The Book Club Connection: Literacy Learning and Classroom Talk* (Teacher College Press) and co-authored *Book Club: A Literature-Based Curriculum*. She is currently (1999) the president-elect of the National Reading Conference and was selected as Outstanding Teacher Educator in Reading in 1996 by the International Reading Association.

Introduction

I want to situate this volume, authored by six Michigan literacy educators, within the national context. For this purpose, I would like to share some of the lessons I have been learning as I complete my first year on the Board of Directors of the International Reading Association. These are my own thoughts, not the official views of the Board or the Association.

An important lesson I have learned is that literacy educators, concerned parents, and others need to become much more actively involved in the political arena. When we leave responsibility for shaping decisions to others who know much less about literacy instruction than we do, we run the risk of seeing events move in directions that may do serious harm to our work with students. At the federal level, a prime example is the initial version of the Reading Excellence Act. As originally proposed, this act would have made federal funding available for programs based on "reliable, replicable research," a phrase intended to support only direct instruction approaches to the teaching of phonics and other skills. This legislation was an attempt both to define what constitutes valid research in literacy and to take curriculum decision-making away from states and districts.

The field of literacy, in common with the broader field of educational research, has long since expanded its repertoire of methodologies to embrace classroom-based, quasi-experimental, naturalistic, qualitative studies, along with quantitative work. This shift has come about in large part because of the realization that schools are complex, dynamic settings, and that the results of studies conducted under idealized laboratory conditions are unlikely to generalize to the real world of classrooms. Furthermore, the field has recognized the value of action research by teachers, based on work in their own classrooms. Literacy educators, parents, and concerned citizens had great cause to be concerned about the narrow view of literacy and research endorsed in the original formulation of the Reading Excellence Act.

In the past, curriculum decision-making, in keeping with the American tradition of states' rights, has been seen as the prerogative of states and districts, not the federal government. From the perspective of literacy education, it makes sense to give responsibility for curriculum decision-making to those closest to the scene: educators who work in the schools, parents, and community members, all of whom have detailed knowledge of the needs of particular groups of students in learning to read. Why should government officials in Washington, DC, dictate literacy curricula for students in Honolulu or Lansing? Yet, in its original form, this was the approach proposed in the Reading Excellence Act. Fortunately, this story did not end badly. Thanks to the diligent efforts of the International Reading Association and other professional organizations, significant changes were made to the Reading Excellence Act prior to its passage.

This was a close call, and it certainly opened my eyes. As a literacy educator, I feel that I need to become more skilled in communicating with policymakers, parents, and the public. I have not spent a great deal of time learning how to communicate my views to these audiences. Yet I have learned that, as literacy educators, we need to get the word out, to relay what we know and understand to those outside of the schools. In getting the word out, we must continue to respect the complexity of literacy and literacy learning, but we must also make it clear that simplistic solutions, such as a return to basics, cannot meet the needs of our students and prepare them for the challenges of tomorrow. This volume, with its clear and concise discussion of issues, serves well as means of communicating with a wide audience. Its message will be helpful not only to classroom teachers, but building principals and school central office staff as well as board members, other policymakers, and the community at large.

Another valuable lesson I have learned is the importance of literacy research in two different areas. First, research can give us good evidence of what constitutes effective literacy instruction. In this volume, the articles by Pearson and Raphael, Diamond, Hiebert, and Hammond are extremely helpful in this regard. Second, research can inform us about the process of change and the formation of the partnerships needed to bring about lasting benefit to students. Research in this area is less common, but equally important. The articles by Edwards and Birdyshaw are valuable contributions that help us understand how partnerships, particularly with parents, can be formed and sustained.

Taken as a whole, the articles in this volume give testimony to the depth of knowledge and expertise available in the state of Michigan because of the presence of these outstanding literacy leaders. Equally important are the partnerships represented in this work. This volume is being produced under the auspices of the Michigan Reading Association, and the authors represent the State Department of Education, universities, and CIERA, a federally-funded research center.

I have had the pleasure of visiting Michigan on several occasions. On my most recent visit I spent two days in the city of Detroit working at an elementary school. As I walked through the halls, I saw students' work posted outside their classrooms. A display case showed colorful ceramic masks, the products of students' participation in an art project. Students filed by me in orderly fashion on their way to and from lunch. Teachers spoke to students respectfully; students replied in the same manner.

I found the principal in this school to be an instructional leader who actively sought out resources to improve her students' reading achievement. She has established partnerships with area universities, community organizations, businesses, and foundations. Despite an unusually busy schedule of events at the school, she took the time to meet with me at length to explain the different steps she was taking to raise reading achievement. Her efforts showed determination and a clear sense of purpose.

I met with the teachers in four small groups to discuss the issues they faced in reading instruction. The teachers expressed concerns about pacing, moving forward to introduce new strategies and skills while providing adequate review and reinforcement to keep students on track. They wanted to better understand how to assess their students' progress in reading in relation to the district's standards. They worried about struggling readers and how to help them progress more quickly. The teachers appreciated the value of high quality literature in the teaching of reading. At the same time, the teachers said that they systematically taught skills, using the lessons in the basal reading program and adding others of their own, to meet their students' needs. I saw one classroom where a teacher had begun to conduct book clubs, and another where the teacher did extensive work with comprehension strategies.

I spoke at an evening meeting organized for the parents at this and two nearby elementary schools. About 350 parents and teachers filled the school's cafeteria to capacity. During a question-and-answer session, parents raised issues that would challenge any reading expert, including motivation to read, homework, dyslexia, and attention deficit disorder. Parents in the audience stood not only to ask questions but to offer advice to one another. One mother discussed the importance of serving as a role model and showing children that you enjoy reading and writing. Another argued for the importance of paying attention to and praising children's efforts to read. A grandmother explained how she had gradually extended the time she spent reading aloud to an active and inattentive grandchild.

What made these observations remarkable to me was the context in which they occurred. The poverty rate in this school was exceedingly high, even for an inner city school. At the time of my visit, political controversy swirled as the Governor of Michigan and the Mayor of the city were in the process of replacing the entire school board and the educational leadership of this very large school system. Even under these challenging conditions, and in these turbulent times, the educators in this school proceeded calmly and purposefully with their work. Teachers taught, children learned, and a community gathered to support its schools. Of course, much work remains to be done to ensure that the children at this school become good readers, but the foundation for success is being laid.

Such success stories, because they build slowly through years of diligent effort, do not make the headlines. But then real change in real schools is not a flashy process; it requires serious thought and dogged determination. Lasting change in literacy achievement comes about when we look at all sides of an issue and arrive at a balanced view, when we are guided by research rooted in classrooms and experiences with children, and when we form partnerships that include rather than exclude. The work presented in this volume shows a deep understanding of these principles. All involved are to be congratulated for their contributions to this fine volume, which shows that Michigan can be an example to the nation for excellence in literacy education.

Kathryn H. Au
Honolulu, Hawaii
March, 1999

Toward a More Complex View of Balance in the Literacy Curriculum

P. David Pearson, CIERA/Michigan State University
Taffy E. Raphael, CIERA/Oakland University

This book focuses on the issues facing teachers, teacher educators, researchers, parents, and administrators as each group attempts to determine the way it can best contribute to current efforts to improve early literacy instruction. Among the greatest current debates in the field is the question, What is a "balanced" early literacy program? **Balance,** a key term of the late 1990s, has advocates from both sides of the aisle—those who wish to infuse balance into whole language programs (e.g., McIntyre & Pressley, 1996) and those who argue that an early code emphasis is the cornerstone of a balanced framework (e.g., Lyon, 1997). Each side claims that they are the balanced parties in this debate. At stake is the experience we provide students as they enter schooling, and—for many—begin the process of learning to read, write, and talk about all kinds of texts. The contributors to this volume want students' experience to be balanced—to focus on a range of texts, build strategies for working with today's texts and other media, and prepare students for a future that includes sources of information we may not even envision today.

This chapter is based, in part, on a chapter in Gambrell, L., & Morrow, L. (Eds.). (1999). *Best practices in literacy instruction.* New York: Guilford Press.

Our focus in this chapter is to try to take this term, balance, from the semantic turf of both extreme positions: (a) those who publicly assert balance while they champion direct instruction and systematic, synthetic phonics; and (b) those who insinuate balance while pushing for a curriculum shrouded in the developmental discourse—the authentic, genuine, natural reading and writing activities of everyday (i.e., not school) communication contexts. We share our professional vision of the concept of balance, guided by three overarching questions: (a) What is this debate all about? (b) What are the dangers in "balance gone astray"? and (c) What is to be done?

What Is the Debate All About?

This debate can be seen as a single debate or a family of narrower debates about issues such as curricular content, nature of texts, forms and focus of teacher preparation, and professional development.

We can think of this debate as a single debate or a family of narrower debates about issues such as curricular content, nature of texts, forms and focus of teacher preparation and professional development, and control over decisions related to all of these areas. Either way, these are not new issues. Debate(s) about the issues have been going on for decades, perhaps centuries. A century ago, the debates were about ABCs (synthetic phonics) versus the analytic phonics (words first, then the letters; Mathews, 1966.) Shortly after World War II, the debate focused on look-say (as exemplified by the classic Dick and Jane readers) versus phonics (see Chall, 1967; Mathews, 1966). In one form or another, the debate has always been about the emphasis during earliest stages of formal reading instruction—**breaking the code** or **understanding what we read** (see Chall, 1967; 1997 for an historical treatment of the debate), or what Chall described as **code-emphasis** versus **meaning-emphasis.**

The code-emphasis side takes a simple view of reading (Gough & Hillinger, 1980): Reading comprehension = decoding + listening comprehension. Those who advocate the simple view argue that since the code (the cipher that maps letters onto sounds) is what students do not know, the sooner they learn it, the better. They want to get phonics and decoding out of the way early so that students can begin to engage in regular reading, by translating letters into the sounds of oral language and then using the same cognitive processes that enable listening comprehension to understand what they read.

The meaning-emphasis side argues that since making meaning is the ultimate goal of reading, it is best to start students off with that very expectation. If teachers offer lots of "scaffolding" to help students determine textual meaning(s), they will, as a natural by-product, acquire the cipher for mapping sounds onto letters. Moreover, in emphasizing meaning, it is crucial to begin on many fronts at once: oral reading activities; shared reading, where teachers and students together read and study a book; writing through pictures, temporary spellings, and other symbols; and so forth. One side says teach them what they do not directly know; the other says bootstrap what they do not know by relying on what they do know. (See Pearson, 1976 for a full treatment of these issues.)

In addition to debating early emphases, the debate has also been about **instructional focus**—whether the growth of each individual *child* or the sanctity of the *curriculum* dominates the decision-making processes of the teacher. One side wants to make sure that each child experiences the optimal curriculum for his or her development. For example, Harste, Woodward, and Burke (1984) talk about approaches that ensure that the child is the primary curriculum informant. At its extreme, this position can require as many curricula as there are children in a classroom. However, more realistically, this position suggests

Those who advocate the simple view argue that since the code is what students do not know, the sooner they learn it, the better. The other side argues that since making meaning is the ultimate goal of reading, it is best to start students off with that very expectation.

One side suggests that there are multiple activities and literacy events within a classroom that children will experience differently depending on where they are in their own literacy development. The other side, while acknowledging the individuality of each reader, emphasizes that every child needs to go through particular stages and acquire certain bodies of knowledge to become a proficient reader.

that there are multiple activities and literacy events within a classroom and that children will experience them differently depending on where they are in their own literacy development. The other side, while acknowledging the individuality of each reader, emphasizes the importance of making sure that each and every child goes through particular stages and acquires certain requisite bodies of knowledge in acquiring reading skill. Put differently, one side argues that there are many paths to reading acquisition, while the other argues that there are many variations in the way the single path is traversed (see Hammond, this volume).

There are also certain "overlays" that complicate the debate by introducing peripheral issues (see Bergeron, 1990). Whole language rhetoric is often shrouded in romanticism, sometimes incorporating aspects of radical individualism, usually couched as a right to academic freedom (Bialostock, 1997; Goodman, 1992), and occasionally hinting at a fundamental distrust of institutions of power and authority, such as governmental agencies and commercial enterprises (Bialostock, 1997; Goodman, Shannon, Freeman, & Murphy, 1988). The rhetoric of those who want to return to more skills and phonics has its own set of "shrouds," many moralistic in character. The argument for a "return" to systematic phonics is sometimes characterized as a return to our national roots (Sweet, 1997) or as a struggle to return the power of literacy to individual children and their families (Honig, 1996). The complexity comes through in the very language used within these different positions (e.g., the argument for individualism and academic freedom is parallel to the argument offered by Honig for the return of literacy to families; for an extended discussion on potential home-school connections, see Edwards, this volume).

What Are the Dangers in Balance Gone Astray?

As each side of the aisle has attempted to appropriate the term "balance," our field has seen a conflating of all sorts of issues and constructs that are not necessarily the property of one side or the other. Thus, on one side of the balance beam, we pile up, along with phonics, other often-related constructs like direct instruction, skills emphasis, ability grouping, formal treatment of genre, and curriculum-centered instructional focus. These constructs are pitted against everything that gets piled up on the other side of the balance beam—literary response, genre study, student-centered curricula, and whole language philosophies (see Figure 1).

Oversimplification actually masks crucial areas literacy educators must balance to effectively teach literacy as a lifelong process.

Figure 1
Balance Out of Control

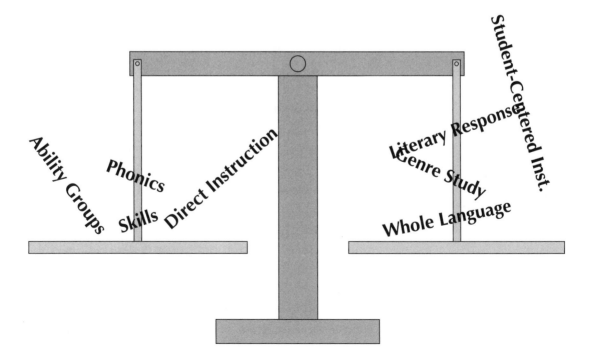

We believe that this oversimplification isn't simply inaccurate, but can actually contribute to a dangerous situation for the field of literacy education, given our current professional context. Specifically, legislative mandates appear to be replacing the marketplace of ideas as the norm in our approach to curriculum change. Enacted (e.g., California Assembly 1086) and proposed (e.g., HR 2614) bills provide strong evidence for this trend. Recently, our field has experienced mandated phonics courses for all teachers (e.g., Ohio, California, Arizona), required phonics for teacher educators (California), and prior approval of the content of inservice programs (California).

This is not to say that the education profession has been immune from legislative mandates in the past. In fact, colleges and universities have long lobbied for particular patterns of coursework as requisite elements of teacher education programs, and they have done so in the name of quality and rigor. What is different now is the specificity of the mandate. It is one thing to have a legislative mandate or an executive order for six or nine hours of coursework in language arts methods; it is quite another thing to mandate the particular philosophical content of the course. While teachers have a long history of responding in varying ways to mandates from every level of policymaking, they have not always run the risk of violating a highly specific law if they did not adopt particular practices.

If highly-specific legislative mandates become the rule, then most—perhaps all—of our values regarding the professionalism of teachers and schooling will be eroded or irretrievably lost. Concepts such as empowerment, professional prerogative, inquiry and reflective practice, agency and intellectual freedom, and local curricular control make sense only under the assumption that what is available to teachers and school communities is a marketplace of research-

If highly specific legislative mandates become the rule, then most—perhaps all—of our values regarding the professionalism of teachers and schooling will be eroded or irretrievably lost.

based ideas from which to make judicious choices about the particular nature of curriculum in our corner of the world. The classic Enlightenment ideal of disseminating knowledge so that enlightened (i.e., informed by our best knowledge and practice) citizens can exercise freedom of choice is a mockery if there are no choices left to make. Notice that, in the bargain, we also compromise the values and practices we have extolled in the recent reform movements (local decision-making, community involvement in schools, ownership). These are high prices to pay for one particular model of research-based practice.

What Is to Be Done?

We think that by unpacking and reassembling this phenomenon we call balance, we can build a case for the rich knowledge bases teachers need in order to implement a truly balanced curriculum. In so doing, we "recomplexify" balance, arguing that there are many independent elements that must be simultaneously balanced. As we unpack this construct, we find it useful to think of a series of continua that reflect the *context* and the *content* of literacy instruction.

Contextual Continua

There are at least four contextual aspects that literacy educators balance in their daily teaching activities (see Figure 2).

First, the notion of **authenticity** has been identified as crucial to students' literacy learning. The argument underlying the promotion of authenticity is that too many school tasks are unauthentic, unrealistic, and, by implication, not useful for engaging in real world literacy activities; that is, instead of teaching kids

The notion of authenticity has been identified as crucial to students' literacy learning. Writing, reading, and talking about text must be grounded in authentic tasks and goals.

Figure 2
Balancing Contextual Factors

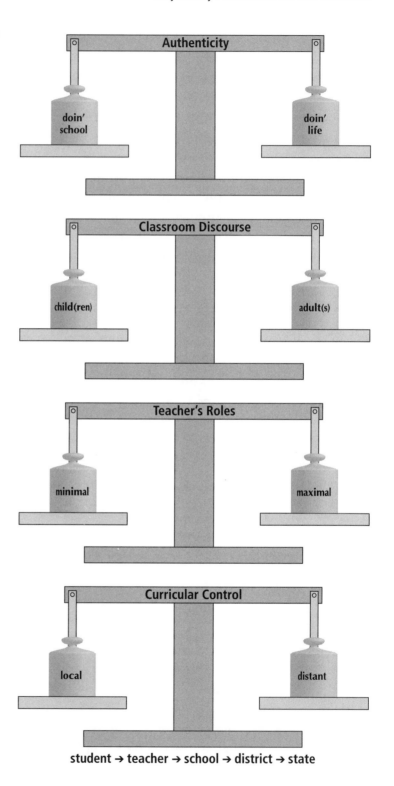

how to "do school," we should be teaching them how to "do life." Writing, reading, and talking about text must be grounded in authentic tasks and goals. These include writing for a real audience and purpose (Bruce & Rubin, 1993) or reading to engage in book club or literacy circle discussions with teachers and peers (e.g., Daniels, 1994; McMahon et al., 1997), rather than writing to demonstrate knowledge of conventions or reading to successfully answer a set of comprehension questions. It may be difficult to find controversy in an emphasis on authenticity. However, if pursued too literally, some useful skills may never be acquired. There may be no occasion, if all instruction is subject to the authenticity criterion, for dealing with formal features of language such as phonics, grammar, and punctuation as objects of study. For example, children arguably need to understand the **code**—how sounds are captured in written language, conventions for conveying stress and intonation—for engaging in lifelong literacy. Yet the practice activities associated with becoming fluent in such areas may be limited to school practice tasks or reading practice readers. Clearly, balance is important across "doing school" and "doing life."

A second contextual aspect is the type of **classroom discourse** students experience. Sociolinguists such as Cazden (1988) and Philips (1972) note the importance of control, specifically over topics and turn-taking. Teachers may control topics and turns, topics but not turns, turns but not topics, or neither topic nor turn. Similar control can be exerted by students. Depending on the goal of the literacy event, activity, or lesson, different patterns of classroom talk are appropriate.

The **teachers' role(s)** within a classroom are closely related to the type of classroom discourse. Au and Raphael (1998) characterize variations in teachers' roles in terms of the amount of teacher control and student activity. They define five teacher roles: (a) explicit instructing, (b) modeling, (c) scaffolding, (d) facilitating, and (e) participating. These reflect decreasing control by the teacher and increased activity on the part of the student (see Figure 3).

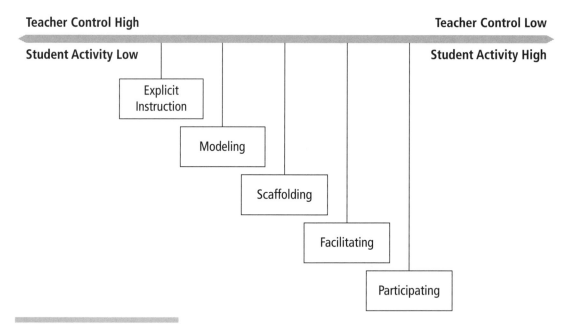

Teacher Control High   **Teacher Control Low**

Student Activity Low   **Student Activity High**

Explicit Instruction

Modeling

Scaffolding

Facilitating

Participating

Figure 3
Teachers' Roles

It is just as incorrect to assume that literacy learning is limited to situations in which the teacher is engaged in explicit instruction as it is to assume that learning is meaningful only when the teacher is out of the picture.

Thus, students are most passive when teachers are engaged in direct instruction, and they are most active when the teacher simply participates with them in the talk of the classroom. Au and Raphael's description implies that it is just as mistaken to assume literacy learning is limited to situations in which the teacher is engaged in explicit instruction as it is to assume that learning is meaningful only when the teacher is out of the picture.

A fourth aspect is that of **curricular control.** At one extreme, control is most distant from the classroom (e.g., at the national or state levels) where curriculum is controlled by those least familiar with the specific students studying the curriculum. Such control may be exerted by mandating textbooks to be used, specifying standards or benchmarks of performance, and so forth. At the other extreme, control is in the hands of those most intimately involved with the students, specifically classroom teachers or grade level teams. Balancing these two extremes is crucial. On the one hand, all educators must make clear those standards to which we would hold our students accountable as they move through the curriculum. Fourth grade teachers have the right to assume that certain curriculum content was covered and mastered prior to students entering grade four. Similarly, the fourth-grade teacher has a right to know what information these students will be held accountable for when they matriculate to their next grade level. However, perhaps only the parents of these fourth graders know them better than their classroom teachers. Thus, to dictate specific instructional methods and even specific curriculum materials for reaching benchmarks and standards is to deny students the right to have those decisions made by the individuals who know them best, their teachers.

Content Continua

Balancing the contextual aspects of literacy instruction sets the stage for balance within the content of what is taught. We highlight three aspects of the curricular content that have been central to debates about literacy instruction: (a) skill contextualization, (b) text genres, and (c) response to literature (see Figure 4).

Skill contextualization reflects the degree to which skills related to our language system, comprehension strategies, composition strategies, and literary analysis are taught within the context of specific texts, either in response to these texts or as invited by them. At one extreme, teachers may rely on a prede-

At one extreme, teachers may rely on a predetermined curriculum of skill instruction. At the other extreme, the curriculum is unveiled as teachable moments occur, with the text and tasks functioning as springboards to skill or strategy instruction. We suggest the need for teachers to operate flexibly between these two extremes.

Figure 4
Balancing Curricular Content

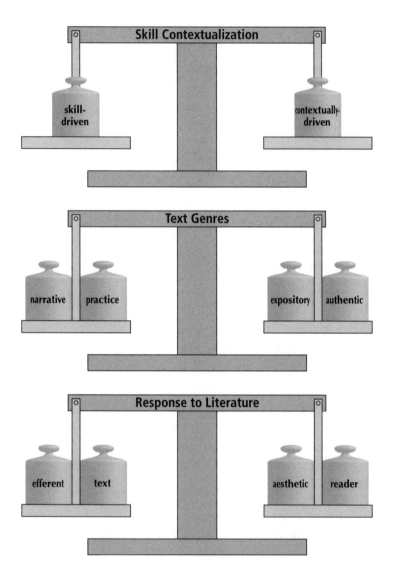

termined curriculum of skill instruction, often tied to a curricular scope and sequence that operates within and across grade levels. At the other extreme, the texts and tasks are the determining force behind what is taught; the curriculum is unveiled as teachable moments occur, with the text and tasks functioning as springboards to skill or strategy instruction.

We suggest the need for teachers to operate flexibly between these two extremes. It makes a great deal of sense, for example, to teach about point of view as students read historical fiction related to the American Civil War, even if point of view happens to be scheduled at some other point in the academic year's guide to curriculum. Conversely, it makes little sense, in the context of reading Bunting's (1994) *Smoky Night* to a group of second graders, to highlight the /fl/ blend in flames, simply because it appeared in the text at the same time that the /fl/ blend popped up in an instructional scope and sequence plan. However, strict reliance on emerging questions, issues, or teachable moments as the standard by which teachers determine the content of the literacy curriculum creates problems or uncertainties; at some point, aspects of the literacy curriculum really do have to be covered.

A second area of content balance is **genre** (see Hicks, 1998; Pappas & Pettegrew, 1998). Genre refers to the types of texts that form the basis of the literacy curriculum—stories, personal narratives, poems, essays, descriptions, and a whole range of specific expository structures. Results of state tests such as the Michigan Educational Assessment Program, as well as the National Assessment of Educational Progress, demonstrate the difficulties students have reading and understanding expository text, especially when contrasted with narrative. While there are different explanations for the source of these disparate scores, there is agreement that young children find informational texts challenging to both read and write (Englert, Stewart, & Hiebert, 1988). In our efforts to balance the curriculum, we must ensure that students have the opportunity and the instructional support necessary to make meaning across the range of genres that exist.

The genre debate also involves authentic versus instructional texts. Some literacy educators argue

In our efforts to balance the curriculum, we must ensure that students have the opportunities and instructional support necessary to make meaning across the range of genres that exist.

that young readers learn best when reading and responding to authentic literature, which contains purposeful use of language, complex natural language, and compelling story lines. Others have argued that such literary criteria make little sense for selecting books that young readers need to become fluent readers (e.g., Hiebert, 1998). Teachers need the flexibility to travel the full range of positions on this axis as well. Even our youngest students must be able to handle, read (even "pretend read"), and respond to high quality literary texts—texts written by authors to inform, persuade, entertain, and inspire. However, when it comes to acquiring the skills that enable authentic reading, relying on literature to promote skill development may serve neither the literature nor the skills well. Factors from word placement on a page to relationships between words and pictures may actually make wonderful literary texts poor materials for practicing and fine-tuning skills. Also, the sheer amount of practice reading that early readers need to engage in calls for a host of easy-to-read books students can read at their independent levels. As engaging as these books may be to young and enthusiastic readers, many, perhaps most, may never qualify as quality literature. Neither high quality trade books nor practice books can serve as the sole diet of books if young readers are to become proficient in literacy activities.

> The sheer amount of practice reading in which early readers need to engage calls for a host of easy-to-read books students can read at their independent levels.

The third dimension of content balance is **response to literature.** The debate here stems from complex issues related to readers' individual interpretations of text and the tensions concerning social and cultural values that almost inevitably arise in literature discussions. This debate has been traveled along two axes— reader-driven versus text-driven understandings, and conventional (i.e., culturally sanctioned) versus personal interpretations. As our field has moved toward authentic literature as the basis for our reading programs, teachers find themselves face to face with students' responses to the content of literature: the enduring themes of the human experience (love, hate, prejudice, friendship, religious values, human rights, and so forth). Fourth and fifth graders reading Taylor's (1990) *Mississippi Bridge* will undoubtedly initiate conversations about how the African-Americans were treated by southern whites in the 1930s, which can lead to conversations about race relations today. Third graders reading and responding to McLerran's (1992) *Roxaboxen* unpack their own family stories and memories, and consider the relationships they have with family members across generations.

Debates about response are deeply rooted in beliefs about the functions of schooling, the separation of church and state, and the roles of parents and teachers. Further, they are rooted in beliefs about the development of students' interpretive dispositions— whether we privilege the readers' interpretation of the story's meaning or author's message, or whether there is a "correct" (official or conventional) meaning that teachers are obligated to help students learn for later demonstration that they have acquired that conventional meaning. Balancing response to literature actually involves balancing the tension between the two goals of schooling—connecting to the past and preparing to meet an uncertain future. On the one hand, schools are obligated to teach students the cultural lore of our society, our history, our cultural and linguistic tools, and our norms for interaction. On the other hand, schools must build our future citizenry, helping students become adults who can live in a world that will undoubtedly differ significantly from the world we live in today. The tension between convention and invention must be addressed through a curriculum that balances individual with culture.

On the one hand, schools are obligated to teach students the cultural lore of our society, our history, our cultural and linguistic tools. On the other hand, schools must build our future citizenry. This tension between convention and invention must be addressed.

Concluding Comment: Rethinking Balance

We borrow from environmental science the concept of **ecological balance,** which suggests a system that works to support each individual component—a curriculum that doesn't pit one aspect against another. In doing so, we hope to suggest that we must shift the debates about balance *away* from single-dimension discussions of what to teach and what not to teach, and *toward* the notion that achieving a balanced literacy curriculum is a logical goal of all literacy educators. The ecologically balanced curriculum that follows is based on research studying a literature-based program, Book Club, for upper elementary reading instruction (Raphael & Goatley, 1994, 1997) and a K–5 literacy curriculum designed for the Kamehameha Early Education Program (Au et al., 1997). Both programs are grounded in the belief that ownership of literacy is central to students' lifelong success (see Au & Raphael, 1998). The literacy instructional content that forms the ecological system consists of

Figure 5
An Ecologically Balanced Curriculum

Comprehension	Composition	Literary Aspects	Language Conventions
Background Knowledge: • prediction Text Processing: • summarizing • sequencing • identifying importance Monitoring: • clarifying • planning	Process: • planning • drafting • revising Writing as a Tool Writing from Sources On-Demand Writing	Literary Elements: • theme • plot • character • setting Response to Literature: • personal • creative • critical	Sound/Symbol Grammar Syntax Interaction

four areas: (a) comprehension, (b) composition, (c) literary aspects, and (d) language conventions (see Figure 5).

Each of these four areas is supported by extensive bodies of research using a range of rigorous research methods (see Raphael & Brock, 1997). We must be conscious not to weigh in too heavily against any particular curriculum aspect, such as downplaying the role of phonics, as depicted in Figure 6.

Nor should we be overly optimistic about teaching only a small part of the curriculum and hoping the rest will follow, as depicted in Figure 7.

Rather, we must recognize that the issue of balance is better described in terms of multiple dimensions of both content and context (see Hammond, Hiebert, this volume). Unpacking the cluster of dimensions in our balance beam metaphor and focusing on the specifics of content and contextual facets that compose reading instruction demonstrate some of the com plexities in that debate. If we allow teachers the prerogative, for particular students and situations, of positioning themselves on each of these scales

> We must recognize that the issue of balance is better described in terms of multiple dimensions of both content and context.

Figure 6
Lack of Balance When Curriculum Is Ignored

Comprehension	Composition	Literary Aspects	Language Conventions
Background Knowledge: • prediction Text Processing: • summarizing • sequencing • identifying importance Monitoring: • clarifying • planning	Process: • planning • drafting • revising Writing as a Tool Writing from Sources On-Demand Writing	Literary Elements: • theme • plot • character • setting Response to Literature: • personal • creative • critical	Grammar Syntax Interaction

independently of the others, then we go a long way toward avoiding the oversimplifications that can so easily overwhelm us in this debate.

Teachers are not simply whole language or skills teachers. Sometimes, for some children, they look like one; other times, for other children, they look like the other. This is because they make conscious, intentional decisions about individual students based upon each of these important dimensions. We believe there is merit in the metaphor of multiple balance beams, each with at least one, and sometimes two, axes that must be traversed thoughtfully and independently. It makes balance a more elusive construct, but also a more powerful one—one that we hope we can all strive to achieve in our teaching.

> Teachers are not simply either whole language or skills teachers. Sometimes, for some children, they look like one; other times, for other children, they look like the other.

Figure 7
Lack of Balance When Curriculum Is Overemphasized

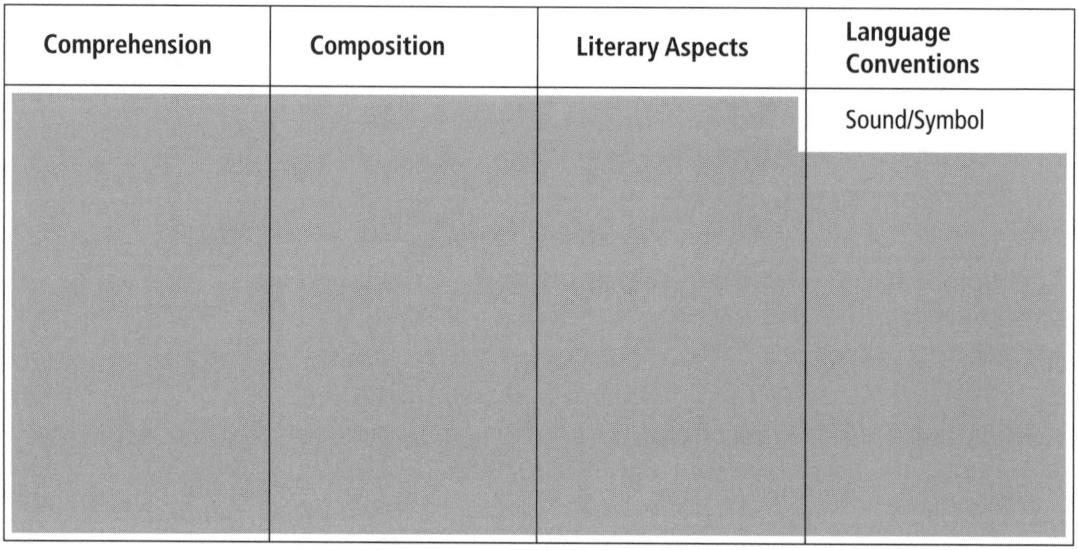

Comprehension	Composition	Literary Aspects	Language Conventions
			Sound/Symbol

References

Au, K. H., Carroll, J. H., & Scheu, J. R. (1997). *Balanced literacy instruction: A teacher's resource book.* Norwood, MA: Christopher-Gordon Publishers.

Au, K. H., & Raphael, T. E. (1998). Curriculum and teaching in literature-based programs. In T. E. Raphael & K. H. Au (Eds.), *Literature-based instruction: Reshaping the curriculum* (pp. 123–148). Norwood, MA: Christopher-Gordon Publishers.

Bergeron, B. S. (1990). What does the term whole language mean? Constructing a definition from the literature. *Journal of Reading Behavior, 22* (4), 301–329.

Bialostock, S. (1997). Offering the olive branch: The rhetoric of insincerity. *Language Arts, 74* (8), 618–629.

Bruce, B. C., & Rubin, A. D. (1993). *Electronic quills: A situated evaluation of using computers for writing in classrooms.* Hillsdale, NJ: Erlbaum.

Bunting, E. (1994). *Smoky night.* San Diego, CA: Harcourt.

Cazden, C. (1988). *Classroom discourse: The language of teaching and learning.* Portsmouth, NH: Heinemann.

Chall, J. S. (1967). *Learning to read: The great debate.* New York: McGraw-Hill.

Chall, J. S. (1997). *Learning to read: The great debate.* (3rd ed.). New York: McGraw-Hill.

Daniels, H. (1994). *Literature circles: Voice and choice in the student-centered classroom.* York, ME: Stenhouse Publishers.

Englert, C. S., Stewart, S. R., & Hiebert, E. H. (1988). Young writers' use of text structure in expository text generation. *Journal of Educational Psychology, 80,* 143–151.

Goodman, K. (1992). Whole language research: Foundations and development. In S. J. Samuels & A. E. Farstrup (Eds.), *What research has to say about reading instruction* (2nd ed.). (pp. 46–69). Newark, DE: International Reading Association.

Goodman, K. S., Shannon, P., Freeman, Y., & Murphy, S. (1988). *Report card on basal readers.* Katonah, NY: Richard C. Owen Publishers.

Gough, P. B., & Hillinger, M. L. (1980). Learning to read: An unnatural act. *Bulletin of the Orton Society, 30,* 171–176.

Harste, J. C., Woodward, V. A., & Burke, C. L. (1984). *Language stories and literacy lessons*. Portsmouth, NH: Heinemann.

Hicks, D. (1998). Narrative discourses as inner and outer word. *Language Arts, 75* (1), 28–34.

Hiebert, E. H. (1998). Selecting texts for beginning reading instruction. In T. E. Raphael & K. H. Au (Eds.), *Literature-based instruction: Reshaping the curriculum* (pp. 195–218). Norwood, MA: Christopher-Gordon Publishers.

Honig, B. (1996). The role of skills in a comprehensive reading program. *California English, 1* (3), 16–20.

Lyon, G. R. (July 10, 1997). Statement before the Committee on Education and the Workforce. Washington, DC: U.S. House of Representatives.

Mathews, M. M. (1966). *Teaching to read: Historically considered*. Chicago: University of Chicago Press.

McIntyre, E., & Pressley, M. (1996). *Balanced instruction: Strategies and skills in whole language*. Boston, MA: Christopher-Gordon Publishers.

McLerran, A. (1992). *Roxaboxen*. New York: Puffin Books.

McMahon, S. I., & Raphael, T. E., with Goatley, V. J., & Pardo, L. S. (Eds.). (1997). *The Book Club connection: Literacy learning and classroom talk*. New York, NY: Teachers College Press.

Pappas, C., & Pettegrew, B. S. (1998). The role of genre in the psycholinguistic guessing game of reading. *Language Arts, 75* (1), 36–44.

Pearson, P. D. (1976). A psycholinguistic model of reading. *Language Arts, 53,* 309–314.

Philips, S. U. (1972). Participant structures and communicative competence: Warm Springs children in community and classroom. In C. Cazden, V. P. John, & D. Hymes (Eds.), *Functions of language in the classroom* (pp. 370–394). New York: Teachers College Press.

Raphael, T. E., & Brock, C. H. (1997). Instructional research in literacy: Changing paradigms. In C. Kinzer, D. Leu, & K. Hinchman (Eds.), *Inquiries in literacy theory and practice* (pp. 13–36). Chicago: National Reading Conference.

Raphael, T. E., & Goatley, V. J. (1994). The teacher as "more knowledgeable other": Changing roles for teaching in alternative reading instruction programs. In C. Kinzer & D. Leu (Eds.), *Multidimensional aspects of literacy research, theory, and practice* (pp. 527–536). Chicago: National Reading Conference.

Raphael, T. E., & Goatley, V. J. (1997). Classrooms as communities: Feature of community share. In S. I. MacMahon & T. E. Raphael (Eds.), *Book Club: Literacy learning and classroom talk* (pp. 26–46). New York: Teachers College Press.

Sweet, R. W. (May/June 1997). Don't read, don't tell. *Policy Review*, 38–42.

Taylor, M. D. (1990). *Mississippi bridge.* New York: Bantam Books.

Every Child a Reader: At Work in a First-Grade Classroom

Elfrieda H. Hiebert, CIERA/University of Michigan

In the summer of 1998, a group of researchers at the Center for the Improvement of Early Reading Achievement (CIERA) conducted a literature review to identify key principles that could guide the development of strong instruction for teaching young children to read, and for helping struggling readers in the early grades. The review resulted in *Every Child a Reader* (Hiebert, Pearson, Taylor, Richardson, & Paris, 1998), a set of guidelines, a summary of research, and bibliographies for further readings. These materials are organized around eight topics, addressing (a) oral language and reading; (b) concepts of print, letter naming, and phonemic awareness; (c) phonics and word recognition accuracy; (d) high-frequency words and fluency; (e) strategic comprehension; (f) writing and reading; (g) engagement and interest in reading; and (h) schoolwide reading programs. In this chapter, I take the reader into "Ben's" classroom,[1] a first-grade classroom in an urban setting, where most of the children live at what by today's standards is considered a poverty level. The children represent diverse ethnic and linguistic groups. All live in an environment where the challenges of day-to-day living are taxing for both adults and children.

The chapter is organized by principle. In each section, I introduce the principle as worded in *Every Child a Reader*. I then elaborate on how this principle is instantiated, using examples from Ben's classroom and from his students.

Topic 1: Oral Language and Reading

Children's oral language abilities are interwoven with learning to read and write. The oral language children acquire as preschoolers helps them to connect words and sounds with print. Throughout the school years, oral language is both a means whereby children learn about reading and a goal of reading instruction.

When children are learning to read and write, they have access to a tool that was not available to them when they learned to talk; this tool is, in fact, their facility with oral language. By the time they reach school, children can use many words in appropriate grammatical structures to communicate their ideas. Many have also discovered the relationship between the language they speak fluently and the written form this language takes. While they may not have grasped the alphabetic principle (i.e., the manner in which oral language maps onto written language), they know that the string of symbols, like the logos of familiar brands, is associated with the ideas they express in talk.

A second way in which oral language functions as a tool for children in learning to read is that adults use oral language to direct children's attention to the critical features of written language and the processes for using written language. For example, a teacher might say to a group, while pointing to the word school on a sign, "The word *school* starts with the letter *s*. Who has a name that starts with the letter *s*? Samantha?" Children also use oral language to get information about written language. They ask, "What does that say? What letter is that? How do you spell Grandma?"

As children become adept at making the associations between oral and written language, talk becomes the means whereby they share their understandings of books and hear how their peers have interpreted these same books. Oral language serves as the means whereby children express their confusions, talk through their new insights, and hear about new features and uses of written language. Ben is aware of research on children's language use and on the ways in which language can be used to invite children to higher levels of participation in tasks (see Gover & Englert, 1998). He builds on this information in selecting books for read-alouds that have challenging content and in the kinds of questions he asks children about the books. For example, earlier in the year, Ben used the book *Quick as a Cricket* (Wood, 1982) for a series of lessons aimed at getting children to attend to words. This book consists of a series of similes about a child, where the child describes himself as "I'm as brave as a tiger," or "I'm as tame as a poodle." The illustrations depict contexts where the attributes of bravery or tameness are appropriately represented. As Ben and his students discuss the story, the children learn to distinguish between different attributes such as tameness and bravery. There are many animals and characteristics that are not used in the everyday talk of Ben's students: basset, or ox, for example. There is also the notion of simile—a figure of speech. Ben raises questions about this language feature (e.g., "What are some other comparisons that you have heard people make?") and about the content of the book (e.g., "Does anybody here have a basset hound? What can you tell me about bassets?")

As children become adept at making the associations between oral and written language, talk becomes the means whereby they share their understandings of books and hear how their peers have interpreted these same books.

Topic 2: Concepts of Print, Letter Naming, and Phonemic Awareness

Two powerful predictors of first-grade reading achievement are letter-name knowledge and phonemic awareness (the conscious awareness of the sounds in spoken words). To apply this knowledge successfully in learning to read, children need to understand the purposes and conventions of reading and writing.

Most of the first graders in Ben's classroom began the school year with an understanding of books, an ability to recognize letters in a meaningful way, and an awareness of the sounds in written language. That was not the case last year, when almost half of the first graders needed the first term of the year to gain fundamental understandings about the purposes of reading and writing and the alphabetic principle.

Ben was instrumental in this shift in the children's knowledge. In this school, children stay together as a class but are not with the same teacher from year to year. Last year, which was Ben's first year in the school, Ben learned from his assessments of the first graders at the beginning of the year that many of the children were not tracking print on a picture book reading task modeled after Sulzby (1985). Too many of the students in his class were telling stories from the pictures and not attending to the print on the page.

One of the first things that Ben did was give the kindergarten teacher a copy of the book *Hey! I'm Reading!* (Miles, 1995). This book served as the means whereby the kindergarten teacher began to have "metacognitive" conversations (Palincsar & Brown, 1984) with the children about what can be read and ways to read. In the section entitled "Some ways to read," the book identifies ways that children can become strategic in their reading, such as getting help from pictures, or matching their good idea with the word on the page or the sign. The kindergarten teacher used this book to initiate discussions with students using words they could already read, such as their names and words on signs (e.g., *stop*). Children began collecting words that, when written on cards, could be organized by initial consonants on a word wall. Ben also shared a copy of *Just Open a Book* (Hallinan, 1995) that furthered the conversation in the kindergarten class about all of the things that the class had learned from books in the kindergarten teacher's daily read-aloud events with them—things about the arctic, from *Mama, Do You Love Me?* (Joosse, 1991), or about birds, from *Feathers for Lunch* (Ehlert, 1990).

These conversations about what can be read were instrumental in making children aware of print. Ben, who had recently completed a Master's program in literacy education, also shared strategies with his kindergarten colleague on research on phonemic awareness. He chose children's literature as the context for these discussions, since children's literature is an interest that he and his colleague share. Ben was particularly enthused when he read Yopp's (1995) article on ways in which children's books can be used to support phonemic awareness. The kindergarten teacher subsequently used books such as *Oh, A-Hunting We Will Go* (Langstaff, 1974) for rhythm and rhyming activities.

Ben also gave his colleague a summary of a project on phonemic awareness that has taken place in Michigan over the past decade (Ayres, 1998). The research on this project resulted in a prize-winning dissertation (Ayres, 1993) which established that kindergartners became more phonemically aware when explicit instruction on the sound system of language followed a semester of experiences with books that have rhythm and rhyme (Yopp, 1995).

The kindergarten teacher had always emphasized letter naming and letter-sound matching, although the typical activities had not necessarily been successful in ensuring that children could integrate their knowledge into the task of reading. Once more, Ben supported his kindergarten colleague in making the process of attending to letters and the association between letters and sounds more concrete for young children by sharing sets of "preformed" letters—in this case, cardboard letters. Ben shared with his colleagues ideas that came out of his Writing Center for the previous year's first graders, who had not had the experiences that would have enabled them to grasp the alphabetic principle as kindergartners. (Ben's Writing Center will be described more fully in Topic 6.) He also shared compositions that children were writing, some little more than the consonants of words such as "IWTMFRH" (I went to my friend's house.). He enthusiastically shared with the kindergarten teacher the progress this student (one whom the teacher had had the previous year) made by midyear when the child wrote: "FOR CriSMiS I Goi a Bice iT Wus BiG (For Christmas I got a bike. It was big.) The evidence of children's knowledge about letter-sound relations from these writing samples aided the kindergarten teacher in implementing similar activities.

As the kindergarten teacher has increased the amount of time children spend in writing messages with preformed letters and pens and paper and reading along in books that encourage attention to segmentation, rhyming, and blending of sounds in words, children are beginning first grade eager to read words on their own. Ben's Writing Center with first graders and the read-alouds and use of books for independent reading move some children to the next stage—recognizing words independently. For those children who

As the kindergarten teacher has increased the amount of time children spend in writing messages with preformed letters and pens and paper and reading along in books, children are beginning first grade eager to read words on their own.

still need more time, the activities provide the means for them to engage in tasks with their peers that foster phonemic awareness, letter naming, and a sense of what reading is.

Topic 3: Phonics and Word Recognition Accuracy

To recognize unfamiliar words when reading, successful beginning readers use phonics (letter-sound associations). Phonics knowledge must be applied to unfamiliar words in reading text and requires monitoring for meaning. To prepare for middle-grade reading, children must augment phonics skills with knowledge of English morphology—meaning units such as roots, prefixes, and suffixes.

Topic 4: High-Frequency Words and Fluency

Proficient readers recognize the vast majority of words in texts quickly, allowing them to focus on the meaning of the text. Since approximately 300 words account for 65% of the words in texts, rapid recognition of these words during the primary grades forms the foundation of fluent reading.

The concepts described in these two principles are the focus of Ben's reading lessons with small groups of his first-grade students, as well as the independent reading and writing activities of center time. The two categories of words are not treated separately in children's reading. After all, children need to be proficient with both types of words in reading any text. Ben also realizes, however, that using common letter-sound patterns in getting the pronunciation and meaning of unknown but common words does not necessarily mean that children are quick and automatic in their reading. There is also a critical group of words (approximately 100) that account for half of the words that children read. These high-frequency words are the function words of English grammar— conjunctions, prepositions, articles, and so on. The letter-sound relations of many of these words emanate from Old English and are not perfect reflections of current English pronunciations.

Ben knows that, if children tediously apply their knowledge of letter-sound patterns to these words, they will be jeopardized in two ways. First, the common letter-sound patterns will not necessarily fit. Second, children will be wasting a great deal of their cognitive capacity, if they need to apply letter-sound knowledge to every one of the highly frequent words each time it appears. For example, in this sentence from Polacco's (1994) *My Rotten Redheaded Older Brother:* "'Bet I can pick more blackberries than you can,' he jeered at me one day," words such as *I, can, more, than, you, at, me,* and *one* are among these highly frequent words that occur in many texts. The goal, by the end of first grade, is for children to be able to devote their energies to figuring out the "high-content" words that give the unique meaning to this sentence—words such as *blackberries* and *jeered.*

Ben makes sure that he designs lessons on particular aspects of these two categories of words and the different strategies that are involved in becoming accurate and automatic readers. In some lessons, Ben emphasizes the common pattern across a group of words, aiding children in realizing that a pattern can be consistent and appear in many common words. For example, the word *day* in the sentence cited from Polacco earlier might become the focus of a lesson as children explore other words that have the *ay* pattern, especially ones with two consonants at the beginning: *clay, gray, play, pray, stay, tray,* and even words with three consonants—*spray* and *stray.*

In addition to *My Rotten Redheaded Older Brother,* Ben has located several little books in which words with *ay* are prominent. Children read these books silently and aloud, chorally as well as individually,

In some lessons, the teacher emphasizes the common pattern across a group of words—aiding children in realizing that a pattern can be consistent and appear in many common words.

during the lesson and in the center activities that follow. They also spell *ay* words at the Writing Center with magnetic letters and write words with this pattern and other patterns with felt pens on acetate slates.

In subsequent lessons, Ben focuses on the rapid reading of a group of high-frequency words—*you*, *at*, and *me*. Ben has the children reread several little books in which these words appear, and has them make their own cards with these words. Children use these word cards and others from their word banks to make sentences which they read to one another. Ben then has the children revisit the familiar books with some instances of these words and has them see how rapidly they can read the text, first silently, and then orally.

There are several characteristics of the instruction that Ben provides that research indicates contribute to the success of his students (Taylor & Pearson, 1998). First, Ben has a curriculum that attends to particular types of word recognition as well as comprehension. While many comprehension lessons occur through daily read-alouds with the entire class, Ben also conducts daily lessons with small groups that share similar levels of reading. These lessons attend to particular content and strategies of word recognition and provide children with immediate feedback from the teacher on their application of this content and these strategies.

> While many comprehension lessons occur through daily read-alouds with the entire class, the teacher also conducts daily lessons with children in small groups who share similar levels of reading ability.

Second, Ben works with his students in manageable groups—groups where Ben can guide students in attending to particular features of print, and where children's needs are met. Ben consistently uses an assessment system with the features of the *Michigan Literacy Progress Profile* (Michigan Department of Education, 1998) to establish his students' accomplishments. These assessments are the basis for establishing the groups in which children receive their focused instruction for a period of time.

Third, Ben gives his students appropriate texts. The texts that Ben chooses for particular groups of students have examples of the words that have been the focus of lessons. These texts are also chosen to be at appropriate reading levels for children. The books are not limited to focus words, because Ben knows that children's interest in topics and the language and illustrations of a text can go a long way toward ensuring that children read and reread a book. However, there are not so many unfamiliar words in a book that children's entire time will be spent attempting new words.

Finally, Ben ensures that independent and pair activities extend children's reading and writing. The Writing Center engages the children in writing, while the Reading Center—featuring tape recordings of books so that children can receive feedback as they reread books—and the instruction that Ben has provided to aid children in reading to one another extend children's reading. Each school day also ends with children's plans for reading after school with books selected.

Topic 5: Strategic Comprehension

The basic comprehension strategies that children build out of oral language skills in kindergarten and first grade become more complex in second grade and beyond. As topics and text structures become less familiar and the goal of reading shifts from understanding familiar ideas to acquiring new information, students must develop strategies for texts that extend beyond their own knowledge base.

When Ben begins the academic year with his first-grade students, he knows that one of the first challenges they face is understanding what a book is about and the relationship between the symbols on the page and what they represent. In short, there is a parallel between what they know and what exists in print. Thus, it is not surprising that a major factor in selecting texts for beginning readers is familiarity. These familiar texts build upon the concepts and the language patterns that young children recognize. The classic *Brown Bear, Brown Bear, What Do You See?* (Martin, 1967) uses a simple repetitive pattern with familiar animals in familiar settings. Fluency is a primary goal: Ben aims to help young readers develop a working knowledge of familiar sight words and a plan for figuring out those words not immediately recognized by sight, using strategies related to context clues and sound/symbol knowledge.

However, if Ben only focuses on fluency, he will not prepare his students for texts they will begin to encounter as they move through school, since texts eventually become the place where new information is acquired. This is true of both narrative and informational books. When Galda (1998) writes about literature, she uses the metaphor that it is a mirror that reflects the familiar back to us for examination and interpretation, but she also points out that is a window into the unfamiliar—distant peoples, places, and times. Over time, increasingly unfamiliar material is encountered by students. Ben begins to prepare his students for less familiar texts early in the school year.

For example, in late fall, Ben introduced his students to a unit focused on learning about sea animals—not a topic immediately familiar to students in mid-Michigan. He began by using the Brown Bear book pattern to study less familiar concepts. For example, he made a chart paper book with pages such as, "Octopus, octopus, what do you see? I see a diver looking at me." The use of familiar patterns with

It is not surprising that a major factor in selecting texts for beginning readers is familiarity. These familiar texts build upon the concepts and the language patterns that young children recognize.

unfamiliar concepts serves as a bridge to using reading skills to develop new knowledge.

A second way that Ben helps his students prepare is by increasing his focus on teaching strategies relevant to learning from new and unfamiliar texts. As a field, we've learned how important background knowledge is to comprehension (Anderson & Pearson, 1984). Before beginning a new book, Ben models ways of approaching the book, using a modification of the Experience-Text-Relationship framework (Au & Kawakami, 1984). He begins by asking questions to elicit relevant experiences from his students' lives. He then asks each student to look at the book and predict what it will be about. He solicits what they know about the topic, knowing that some of their experiences may have been passive, such as from watching television, but are nonetheless relevant to the text. He asks students to consider the words they might anticipate seeing. Before reading a book about sea animals, he asked them what words they thought they might see (e.g., ocean, shark, dolphin, coral).

A third way Ben prepares his students to read independently is by introducing students to a range of text processing strategies, from sequencing to identifying main ideas. He does this early on with highly familiar story lines. Again, new strategies are more easily learned in the context of highly familiar text content. He then slowly introduces them to increasingly unfamiliar content, while helping them apply strategies they have learned. For example, he read *The Magic Maguey* (Johnston, 1996), a story set in a Mexican pueblo—clearly an unfamiliar context to many, if not all, of his students. However, the story was one that many students could identify with: the tale of a young boy who saves a treasured maguey bush through his cleverness. There are many points of connection in the story, as well as potential points of disconnection.

As a field we've learned how important background knowledge is to comprehension. Before beginning a new book, the teacher asks the students questions to elicit relevant experiences. He or she solicits what the children know and asks them to predict what the book might be about.

New strategies are more easily learned in the context of highly-familiar text content.

Before reading the story aloud, Ben uses the brilliant illustrations in the book to help build a sense of the story's sequence. For instance, one illustration shows how leaves from the bush are used to make a roof for their home; in another, the maguey leaves are dried and the threads are used to make a shirt for the main character. Later, a rich man decides to tear down the bush and build his house on that spot. Miguel convinces his friends to help him decorate the bush as a Christmas tree, and all dance and sing joyfully around it, including the rich man. In the end, the rich man decides not to build his house and all live happily ever after. Simply establishing this sequence of events provides a great deal of structure for students' comprehension, and introduces them indirectly to the concept of a story map and the problem-solution structure. Bringing in their own experiences at having helped someone or something in their life helps them make the connection between their own lives and Miguel's, despite differences in culture, country, and characters populating the story.

Fourth, Ben asks questions that help his students reflect on what they're reading, rather than simply correcting their mistakes. Ben often walks around the room during students' silent reading, stopping to maintain informal running records. Greg was reading the sentence, "See the funny little car," but he said *care* for *car*. Following the guidelines as identified in *Every Child a Reader* (Hiebert et al., 1998), Ben responded by asking, "What does that mean?" Notice how this helps signal that an error has been made and gives Greg a chance to self-correct. After Greg does, in fact, self-correct, Ben asks, "How did you know your reading didn't make sense?" This supports Greg's ownership over the reading process, which is fundamental to students' literacy success (Au & Raphael, 1998).

Topic 6: Writing and Reading

Learning to write assists children in their reading; in learning to read, children also gain insights that help them as writers. But writing is more than an aid to learning to read; it is an important curricular goal. Through writing children express themselves, clarify their thinking, communicate ideas, and integrate new information into their knowledge base.

Had Ben begun teaching when I did (two decades ago), his classroom would not have been as full of writing occasions. The two decades that span my initiation as a teacher and Ben's have been full of research on how early participation in writing engages children in literacy. In particular, research has demonstrated how involvement in writing contributes to reading acquisition—especially the "basic skills" that are often seen as the gateways or obstacles to successful word recognition. Indeed, research indicates that extensive writing opportunities aid young children in acquiring the alphabetic principle and in mastering specific letter-sound relationships.

Research has demonstrated how involvement in writing contributes to reading acquisition—especially the "basic skills" that are often seen as the gateways or obstacles to successful word recognition.

Ben's classroom is full of writing events designed to meet the dual goals of helping students become better writers and more sophisticated readers. Key events and contexts in the school day include the Morning Message and the Writing Center. The school day begins with a Morning Message in which Ben serves as the scribe and children contribute important information about their lives at home and at school. For example, on the Tuesday following Martin Luther King, Jr.'s birthday, students in Ben's classroom shared ways they had celebrated his birthday. The Morning Message began with Derek's contribution. He said "I went to church. There were drummers and lots of singing." At the board, Ben asked his students how he should write this for Morning Message, eliciting their response to use Derek's name, rather than the pronoun *I*, since once it was written, they may not remember who had contributed the experience to the message. Ben asked Derek to spell his name so he could write it down. He then asked the class as a whole what letter he should put at the beginning of *went*. After they responded, he completed the word. He then had another student spell the word *to* and he completed the sentence writing *church*. He then asked what mark he should put at the end, eliciting "period." In short, Morning Message served as an opportunity for collaboratively creating a message, practicing spelling and punctuation, and having a conversation to mark the reason for the school holiday.

The Writing Center—a table with supplies such as pens, pencils, preformed letters (e.g., magnetic, styrofoam), various sizes and shapes of papers—is nestled in the back corner of the classroom. At the Writing Center, students engage in writing on self-selected as well as teacher-prompted pieces. As is typical of many of today's classrooms, Ben's students become accustomed over time to publishing their writing for others to read. A common topic for first-grade students is, not surprisingly, writing about themselves. For example, Jennifer has published a three-page book about things she likes. She communicates her ideas effectively, integrating her knowledge of sound/symbol relationships learned in activities such as Morning Message, and her use of patterned writing, familiar to her from books she's heard and read in class events.

The pattern Jennifer uses follows, albeit loosely, from words synonymous with "I like." The first page has a picture of Jennifer in her bed; another shows her watching her mom play softball (see Figure 8). She likes collecting "rox;" she loves her bed because it is "cuftlbl" (comfortable), revealing knowledge of beginning, medial, and ending consonant sounds, and the short vowel sound, /u/.

Topic 7: Engagement and Interest in Reading

From the earliest storybook reading with an adult and the first proudly scribbled message, children enjoy reading and writing because of the social communication and signs of cognitive competence the activities provide. The key to attaining and using literacy, even when sustained effort and attention are needed, is the sense of personal pride that children feel when they succeed.

The teacher is working on several fronts at once, helping his students learn to attend to words and letters, act strategically as they construct meaning, and learn about reading and writing different kinds of texts.

As this chapter illustrates, Ben is working on several fronts at once, helping his students learn to attend to words and letters, act strategically as they construct meaning, and learn about reading and writing different kinds of texts. Underlying all of these efforts is Ben's commitment that children value and enjoy reading and writing. Sometimes, children's participation as readers is described as a function of "motivation" (Maehr, 1984). Often, however, the lack of motivation on the part of first graders in reading and writing can be traced to students' lack of understanding of the purpose of a given task and its relationship to books and writing.

Figure 8
A Page From Jennifer's Book

When children are asked to do tasks that isolate the purposes of reading and writing, especially when their involvement in literacy has been limited, they may appear to be "unmotivated." In fact, they may simply not know why, for example, distinctions between letters are important. When a class is comprised of many children whose reading and writing experiences originate primarily from school—as is the case with Ben's class—immersing children in events that convey the joy and value of reading and writing must remain the first priority.

Immersing children in events that convey the joy and value of reading and writing must remain the first priority.

There are three ways in which Ben ensures that literacy "lives" in his classroom: (a) a literate environment; (b) extensive, diverse reading opportunities; and (c) engaging literacy instruction, ensuring that children are eager to read and write.

The presence of a literate environment is evident from the moment one steps into Ben's classroom. Some of the shelves of books in the Reading Center make it possible for children to see the colorful illustrations on the book jackets. Different books are featured at the Writing Center at particular times, but favorites—books that have been read in read-alouds or read in lessons—occupy a special space. During the first part of the school year, Ben has found that children with limited book access gravitate to familiar books (Martinez & Teale, 1988). Not only are the books important, but so is the degree to which the area itself is inviting. For example, Ben has placed a comfortable beanbag chair at the Reading Center that children are eager to use during center time.

Children's compositions—which for some are drawings with teacher-written labels at the beginning of the year—are published at the entry of the classroom with a sign to all that "We are a class of writers." The Writing Center, discussed earlier, invites children to write in the style of their favorite books, create new and innovative stories, and share stories about their own lives—activities that are motivating and interesting to young writers.

The extensive, diverse reading opportunities Ben provides also motivate the students. These include listening to others' stories, reading with peers in small groups and pairs, reading with student volunteers from upper grades in the school, and reading on their own.

Ben reads aloud daily—often more than once a day—for a variety of purposes. Sometimes he reads from books that relate thematically to subject areas students are studying (e.g., learning about ourselves, learning about the community), or areas they are interested in pursuing (e.g., the environment, dinosaurs). Sometimes the books are illustrative of the wonderful literature available, such as *Smoky Night* (Bunting, 1994) or *Grandfather's Journey* (Say, 1993). Sometimes he reads to calm students down: after lunch, for example, or after recess. In addition to Ben's read alouds, he has created a library of books on tape; some are commercially prepared, but many are performed by volunteers (e.g., parents; children from upper grades who rehearse and record the story, then "present" it to his classroom as a gift). These volunteers are guided in how to read, including using voices where there is cadence and interest, and a pace that allows the first grader to follow along.

Students benefit from extensive opportunities to read themselves. There is guided reading, paired and buddy reading, and individual reading.

Students also benefit from extensive opportunities to read themselves. There is guided reading—books that are used to teach students specific aspects of the reading process; paired and buddy reading, which involves practicing skills and strategies as they reread books from their reading program or explore new books of their choice; and individual reading, a familiar context known as (among other things) sustained silent reading (SSR) and Drop Everything and Read (DEAR).

Finally, in Ben's school, he has the advantage of having developed successful working relationships across grade levels, so that children from the fourth- and fifth-grade classrooms, often struggling readers themselves, rehearse and prepare to read with their first grade "buddies." The motivation comes not from any one of these experiences or opportunities, but from the very fact that there are so many different ways to engage in literate behaviors, with all levels of support and encouragement, across the course of the day.

The contexts for reading, and those for writing described earlier, underscore Ben's commitment to creating interesting and meaningful ways for his students to engage with print. Whether playing with poetry, collaboratively developing a Morning Message, participating in guided reading, or sharing writing, the instructional aspect of the literacy program is engaging, and the texts that he chooses to highlight are interesting.

Whether playing with poetry, collaboratively developing a Morning Message, or participating in guided reading or sharing writing, the instructional aspect of the literacy program is engaging.

Topic 8: Schoolwide Reading Programs

In schools that are successful in fostering high levels of reading achievement, all adults in the school work together on the reading program, build systematic program links across the grades, accept responsibility for all children, and closely monitor students' progress.

A schoolwide reading program has two crucial features. First, it is a shared curriculum that specifies how early literacy behaviors move into later, independent behaviors. Second, there are shared goals across grades, with attention to how changes at one grade level can and should affect the curriculum in later grades. For example, if there is an early intervention

Where no schoolwide program exists, teachers and administrators may create one. An administrator may begin staff development efforts among teachers across grade levels, in order to bring the literacy educational goals of the school into focus and identify specific routines and practices to implement within and across grades. Conversely, teachers may act individually to build a schoolwide program through grassroots efforts.

such as Reading Recovery which is specific to first grade, thought is given to how a greater number of children's improved progress and success at first grade will change the second- and third-grade program.

Where no schoolwide program exists, teachers and administrators may create one through three different efforts. First, an effort can be made through commercially prepared programs that cut across grade levels, though it is important to realize that adopting such a program does not guarantee that it will be effective or appropriate for a particular school. Second, an administrator may begin staff development efforts among teachers across grade levels, to bring the literacy educational goals of the school into focus and identify specific routines and practices to implement within and across grades. Third, teachers may act as individuals to build a schoolwide program through more grassroots efforts.

Ben's principal has emphasized students' achieving high levels of reading, and has relied on a commercially prepared schoolwide textbook program adopted for all grades in the school. However, when Ben began the year, he noted that his students—like many he had read and heard about in his Master's degree studies (Hiebert, 1998)—could not read the texts in the first-grade program. Furthermore, he found that the textbook curriculum was too diffuse, consisting of literally pages of activities to go with each story the students read, but with no overarching framework or rationale that helped him focus his teaching. Ben's situation is typical in that the adopted text materials are relied upon to provide the needed schoolwide focus, while the textbook is in fact more of a resource that supports a well-articulated schoolwide program.

Staff development efforts would help Ben and his colleagues to bring focus to the school-adopted program. In the absence of an effort driven by the administration, Ben has worked hard on a variety of fronts to help create a schoolwide program in his school. Earlier, I described Ben's support of the kindergarten teacher in his school, and the value in doing so for helping students begin first grade with a sounder foundation in concepts of print. In this effort and in designing his first grade program, he drew on an early intervention program directed at small groups (Hiebert et al., 1992; Hiebert & Raphael, 1998) that he learned as part of his Master's program. The important part of this intervention program is the presence of "routines"—that is, a consistent set of activities for lessons that revolve around reading and rereading of texts, writing and spelling words and texts, and word study (see Hiebert & Taylor, in press). These routines have assisted Ben in two important ways. First, they have helped create a predictable structure to the school day for himself and his students, within which important literacy events, activities, and lessons are embedded. Second, he is able to frame his instructional efforts more clearly when he talks with colleagues both informally, as in his interactions with the kindergarten teacher, and more formally, as in staff meetings. In short, the routines help both children and teachers focus on learning and teaching literacy.

Ben is a key source for grassroots efforts in his school, and he has learned how important support from other professional colleagues is to his efforts. He has elected to become part of professional organizations and educational settings that provide support for his commitment to high levels of reading acquisition among children in a high-poverty community. He does not like to rely only on conversations in his school, since they can sometimes be discouraging.

The important part of this intervention program is the presence of "routines"—consistent sets of activities for lessons.

For example, some of the second- and third-grade teachers may maintain traditional grouping patterns and curriculum content that are no longer appropriate, given the levels of achievement children reached in first grade. Thus, with his school colleagues, Ben is part of an informal network of colleagues who interact periodically through email. He also participates in summer institutes, offered through the local university or his school district. He is an active member of the Michigan Reading Association and attends the annual conference.

Whatever the form efforts toward a schoolwide program take, there are consistent features of reading efforts that have been effective (Taylor & Pearson, 1998). First, there must be a clear and focused curriculum. Second, there must be consistent small-group instruction. Third, there must be daily opportunities to read and write. Administrators must support the development of schoolwide programs, since even the best grassroots efforts in the early grades will fade over time if not supported and extended as students continue in their schooling.

> First, there must be a clear and focused curriculum. Second, there must be consistent small-group instruction. Third, there must be daily opportunities to read and write.

Concluding Comment

The eight principles detailed in *Every Child a Reader* are crucial for getting all students off to the right start (see Hiebert et al., 1992). Children will benefit from our widespread efforts to ensure that these principles are in place in the early reading curriculum, and understood and supported throughout the school curriculum.

Notes

The work reported herein was supported under the Educational Research and Development Centers Program, PR/Award Number R305R70004, as administered by the Office of Educational Research and Improvement, U.S. Department of Education. However, the comments do not necessarily represent the positions or policies of the National Institute of Student Achievement, Curriculum, and Assessment or the National Institute on Early Childhood Development, or the U.S. Department of Education, and you should not assume endorsement by the federal government.

1. The descriptions of this classroom are based on the activities of a Michigan teacher. The teacher has been given a pseudonym and, in some instances, activities that the author has observed in other classrooms and read about in the research literature have been integrated.

References

Anderson, R. C., & Pearson, P. D. (1984). A schema-theoretic view of basic processes in reading comprehension. In P. D. Pearson, R. Barr, M. Kamil, & P. Mosenthal (Eds.), *Handbook of reading research* (Vol. 1), (pp. 255–293). New York: Longman.

Au, K. H., & Raphael, T. E. (1998). Curriculum and teaching in literature-based programs. In T. E. Raphael & K. H. Au (Eds.), *Literature-based instruction: Reshaping the curriculum* (pp. 123–148). Norwood, MA: Christopher-Gordon Publishers.

Au, K. H., & Kawakami, A. J. (1984). Vygotskian perspectives on discussion processes in small group reading lessons. In P. L. Peterson, L. C. Wilkinson, & M. Hallinan (Eds.), *The social context of instruction: Group organization and group processes* (pp. 209–225). New York: Academic Press.

Ayres, L. R. (1993). The efficacy of three training conditions on phonological awareness of kindergarten children and the longitudinal effect of each on later reading acquisition. Unpublished doctoral dissertation, Oakland University.

Ayres, L. R. (1998). Phonological awareness training of kindergarten children: Three treatments and their effects. In C. Weaver (Ed.), *Reconsidering a balanced approach to reading* (pp. 209–255). Urbana, IL: National Council of Teachers of English.

Galda, L. (1998). Mirrors and windows: Reading as transformation. In T. E. Raphael & K. H. Au (Eds.), *Literature-based instruction: Reshaping the curriculum* (pp. 1–11). Norwood, MA: Christopher-Gordon Publishers.

Gover, M., & Englert, C. S. (1998). *Orchestrating the thought and learning of struggling writers* (CIERA Report #1-002). Ann Arbor: CIERA/University of Michigan.

Hiebert, E. H. (1998). *Text matters in learning to read* (CIERA Report #1-001). Ann Arbor, MI: CIERA/University of Michigan.

Hiebert, E. H., Colt, J. M., Catto, S., & Gury, E. (1992). Reading and writing of first-grade students in a restructured Chapter 1 program. *American Educational Research Journal, 29,* 545–572.

Hiebert, E. H., Pearson, P. D., Taylor, B. M., Richardson, V., & Paris, S. G. (1998). *Every child a reader: Applying reading research in the classroom.* Ann Arbor: CIERA/University of Michigan.

Hiebert, E. H., & Raphael, T. E. (1998). *Early literacy instruction.* Orlando, FL: Harcourt Brace College Publishers.

Hiebert, E. H., & Taylor, B. M. (in press). Beginning reading instruction: Research on early interventions. In M. Kamil, P. Mosenthal, P. D. Pearson, & R. Barr (Eds.), *Handbook of reading research* (Vol. 3). Hillsdale, NJ: Erlbaum.

Maehr, M. L. (1984). Meaning and motivation: Toward a theory of personal investment. In R. Ames & C. Ames (Eds.), *Research on motivation in education* (Vol. 1) (pp. 115–144). New York: Academic Press, Inc.

Martinez, M. G., & Teale, W. H. (1988). Reading in a kindergarten classroom library. *The Reading Teacher, 41,* 568–572.

Michigan Department of Education. (1998). *Michigan literacy progress profile.* Lansing: Michigan Department of Education.

Palincsar, A. S., & Brown, A. L. (1984). Reciprocal teaching of comprehension-fostering and comprehension-monitoring activities. *Cognition and Instruction, 1,* 117–175.

Sulzby, E. (1985). Children's emergent reading of favorite storybooks: A developmental study. *Reading Research Quarterly, 20,* 458–481.

Taylor, B. M., & Pearson, P. D. (December 1998). School factors contributing to growth in early reading achievement: Quantitative analyses. Paper presented at the annual meeting of the National Reading Conference, Austin, TX.

Yopp, H. (1995). Read-aloud books for developing phonemic awareness: An annotated bibliography. *The Reading Teacher*, *48*, 538–543.

Children's Books Cited

Bunting, E. (1994). *Smoky night.* San Diego, CA: Harcourt Brace.

Ehlert, L. (1990). *Feathers for lunch.* New York: Greenwillow Books.

Hallinan, P. K. (1995). *Just open a book.* Nashville, TN: Ideals Children's Books.

Johnston, T. (1996). *The magic maguey.* San Diego, CA: Harcourt Brace.

Joosse, B. M. (1991). *Mama, do you love me?* San Francisco: Chronicle Books.

Langstaff, J. (1974). *Oh, a-hunting we will go.* New York: Atheneum.

Martin, B. (1967). *Brown bear, brown bear, what do you see?* New York: Henry Holt.

Miles, B. (1995). *Hey! I'm reading!* New York: Alfred A. Knopf, Inc.

Polacco, P. (1994). *My rotten redheaded older brother.* New York: Aladdin Paperbacks.

Say, A. (1993). *Grandfather's journey.* Boston: Houghton Mifflin.

Wood, A. (1982). *Quick as a cricket.* New York: Child's Play.

Diversity in a Democratic Society: Implications for Literacy Instruction

Barbara J. Diamond, Eastern Michigan University

In the undergraduate reading/language arts methods course I teach, one of my first assignments is an autobiography which I initially used to encourage students to reflect on the backgrounds and experiences that have shaped their lives. Ultimately, I want them to understand that who they are—both socially and culturally—will determine how they view their students and shape their classroom practice.

However, I have found that these autobiographies are crucial in the way they help me plan and implement my own teaching. As I read them, I learn about my students' own communities—rural, urban, suburban—and the varied social, cultural, and educational experiences they've had. Some have grown up with diverse populations; others have no experience with diversity. Some have known warm and supportive family relationships; others have had many obstacles to overcome—poverty, a dysfunctional father, an alcoholic mother—along with the related social stigmas. Some students faced challenges navigating the academic world because of learning, physical, and/or emotional disabilities, or because of their race, culture, or linguistic backgrounds. African-American and Latino/a students shared times when they felt on the outside of many of the stories and texts that they read, and told how they felt ignored, isolated, and marginalized by teachers and other school personnel.

Despite varied backgrounds and personal differences, the students' classroom literacy learning experiences were strikingly similar. For example, they all learned to read by the basal approach. Most remember phonics instruction, using workbooks and worksheets, and Science Research Associates (SRA) kits. Students noted that most reading in class was driven by turn-taking in basal reading groups, not by an effort to make reading and discussing literature an integral part of their literacy programs. I wondered why, with all their differences, my students had been taught with one literacy approach, particularly given the fact that, as Spiegel (1998) reports, most literacy approaches work for some children (Adams, 1990; Pflaum, Walberg, Karegianes, & Rasher, 1980), but no one approach works for all children (Calfee & Piontkowski, 1981; Delpit, 1988). Typically, teacher educators have taught literacy education approaches based on sound theory and research, but have often placed less emphasis on diverse learners and the need to combine or modify approaches to meet their needs. Therefore, many teachers have limited and fleeting knowledge about diverse student populations. Moreover, many teachers unwittingly continue to teach *all* students as they themselves were taught in elementary school and are unsure about what recourse they have when these more traditional practices fail.

Teachers need to learn as much as possible about their students' cultural and linguistic backgrounds, as well as their communities, to develop effective literacy practices. Teachers will then be able to develop multiple perspectives on the teaching of literacy—a balanced approach—in order to more adequately meet the needs of their students.

> Teachers need to learn as much as possible about their students' cultural and linguistic backgrounds, as well as their communities, to develop effective literacy practices.

In this chapter, I begin with a discussion of the challenges and opportunities of cultural diversity, followed by an examination of the early literacy socialization of diverse groups. Next, I examine the challenges faced by and needs of the new immigrant population and of second language learners. I then discuss the conditions of students who are poor. Finally, I target learners of diverse academic abilities who cross racial, cultural, and socioeconomic lines. For teachers to develop and teach literacy effectively, they must develop multiple perspectives on all learners, and ultimately adopt a balanced literacy approach.

The Challenge and Opportunity of Cultural Diversity

Carlos[1] was born in the United States and spoke proficient English, even though his mother, a recent immigrant from Mexico, spoke very limited English. Carlos eagerly looked forward to the first day in his new school in a north Detroit suburb. Carlos reflects on these early experiences in his school from the vantage point of a college sophomore. In his essay (Manjarrez, 1991), he shares how acutely aware he was of his differences, even as he suppressed his thoughts:

> Though I was still confused as to who I was, serious questioning was suppressed, and I turned to my studies and sports for acceptance. I would always fall short of raising the question, maybe because I was afraid of the answer....
>
> "O.K. class we have time for a couple questions before we say the pledge of allegiance and go home—Carlos, what is your question?"
>
> "Teacher, why isn't there anyone here who looks like me? Not even the pictures in our books look like me. Teacher, are you like me? Do you eat warm frijoles when you get home? Does your family welcome you into the

home with a language so sweet that you would think it was made for lovers? Teacher, I'm not sure who I am or whether or not I belong here."

"I'm sorry Carlos, we can't discuss your questions today."

One of the fondest memories I have of those days was when my third-grade teacher, Ms. Hopling, told my mother that someday her son would be a writer. Everything then was a playful challenge, and all challenges were met head-on. (p. 31)

In this excerpt, Carlos's feelings of alienation are apparent as he *perceives* that his teacher was insensitive to his needs (even though this may not have been the case). However, his ability to learn was adversely affected by his discomfort in the classroom. As he attempted to adjust to school, acquire literacy skills, and deal with the complexities of diversity, Carlos was overwhelmed. He pulled away from his friends and his grades began to suffer. In time, he was labeled a poor student, though he was promoted in each grade. No one required anything of him, except Mrs. Hopling, who Carlos recalls, "in her very nice way. . . gave me a sort of pep talk on school and trying harder" (p. 56). He described her as being a person who cared.

Carlos's experiences parallel those of many students of diverse cultural backgrounds who find that they are different from the mainstream European-American population. His presence provided a challenge and an opportunity for his teachers. According to Carlos, only Mrs. Hopling met this challenge. Carlos eventually learned about his heritage, developed a love for reading and writing, and achieved academic success. (He is a doctoral student in sociology at Northwestern University at the time of this writing.)

There are ever increasing numbers of children like Carlos from diverse ethnic, racial, and linguistic groups who reside in the United States and who populate our schools. Significantly, the 1990 census reports that 25% of the people in the United States classified themselves as non-European-American. When children are included in these statistics, the percentage is even higher. Current immigration patterns and the birthrates of minority groups have led to estimates that, by the year 2000, both Hispanic-American and Asian-American populations will have grown by more than 20%. The African-American population is estimated to have grown by 12%. In fact, by the year 2000, people of color will compose one-third of all students enrolled in public schools (Hodgkinson, 1985; Littman, 1998). Moreover, authorities project that by 2020, they will compose 46% of the school population (Cushner, McClelland, & Safford, 1992; Littman, 1998).

Given these trends, educators are concerned that the gap between the school literacy achievement of poor culturally and linguistically diverse students and mainstream students has widened (Au, 1998; Ladson-Billings, 1994). Schools and teachers are faced with finding ways to address the challenges and opportunities that linguistic and cultural diversity bring.

Neito (1996) asserts that a culturally relevant literacy curriculum can energize students and make them excited because it focuses on important experiences in their lives. It is not enough, however, for teachers to simply accept cultural differences; they must understand that cultural differences may influence how students learn. Providing a variety of literacy experiences, building on oral language activities—storytelling, choral reading, and dramatic interpretations, combined with "real" books from which to develop specific decoding and comprehension skills—can be an effective method for developing literacy achievement for students of diverse cultural backgrounds. These practices are compatible with

Educators are concerned that the gap between the school literacy achievement of poor culturally and linguistically diverse students and mainstream students has widened.

the students' home experiences and their early literacy socialization patterns.

Early Literacy Socialization

In this section I discuss the literacy socialization of two groups: European-Americans and recently-arrived Mexican-Americans. It is important to note, however, that not all families within these groups experience socialization patterns in the same way. There are variations within, as well as among, groups.

Children from mainstream middle-class European-American culture often experience early language development replete with opportunities to interact with adults. Thus, literacy begins at an early age, as children interact with family to meet personal needs, gain a sense of identity, and establish behavior patterns that reflect cultural values and beliefs (Heath, 1989; Schieffelin & Ochs, 1986; Wertsch, 1991). Mothers, the primary caregivers within this culture, encourage their children to be communicative partners, as they take the child's perspective while reading stories aloud, participating in storytelling activities, and engaging in labeling and question-and-answer routines. These interactions with print parallel the reading and writing experiences of traditional school learning.

Children in recently-arrived Mexican-American families experience caregiving that is provided by both family members *and* close friends. Early literacy experiences are marked by a real sense of community, with oral language and storytelling figuring prominently in the lives of young children. Stories are told as entertainment and as a way of teaching lessons to the young. As stories are told, Mexican-Americans are able to keep alive important cultural and moral values, such as showing respect and politeness toward elders (Heath, 1989). Although children grow up in an environment that is rich with conversation, children are not called upon to give accounts of daily experiences and events, and they learn to use language with little intervention from their parents and adult relatives. Mothers typically do not engage in labeling exchanges, and when they do it is rarely to teach vocabulary (Faltis, 1997). Reading to children is most often experienced when older siblings read to younger children, or when children "play school" with other children (Faltis, 1997).

While important literacy behaviors are embedded in both types of family groups, the contrasts between the groups' language development and early storybook experiences is striking. These differences become significant when we consider the degree of compatibility of each group's literacy behaviors with the literacy instruction taking place in today's schools. Research shows that children whose home lives and primary social networks are consistent with the expectations and styles of the school's have a distinct scholastic advantage (Comer, 1984; Au, 1998). In a classroom in which the teachers are informed decision makers, they understand the differences in home literacy and make adjustments to fit the needs of learners in all cultural groups.

While important literacy behaviors are embedded in both types of family groups, the contrasts between the groups' language development and early storybook experiences are striking.

The New Immigrant Population

In addition to the students of diverse cultural backgrounds, there are increasing numbers of immigrants who arrive daily and are immediately placed in our schools. Vangchai Sayarath, a Laotian fifth grader, is one such student. In his journal, he recounts his family's escape from Thailand to Laos. His family ultimately moved to a midsized city in Michigan. Vangchai writes:

It has been hard for me to move to another country because I do have a difficult time here. When I first came to America, I thought I would live a happy life but I was wrong. Some people would make fun of me just because I am from a different world and it is hard to live like that. Some people would think that I am Chinese just because I look like them. Just think about it. Would you like living your life in a new country with people from different worlds and going to new places? … I have learned from writing about my life that the human spirit is stronger than anything and it does not matter how you look, or how healthy, or how strong you are. It is the human spirit that counts. I have learned another thing. It is that dreams come true if you hope for it and never let go of that dream. (Diamond & Moore, 1995, pp. 361–362)

Immigrant children like Vangchai often experience dissonance as they adjust to a new country. They have not always been safe and happy in their home country, but they understood the ways of their people, the expectations of adults, how to communicate with others (adults and children), how to behave in school, and the many aspects of everyday life that we often take for granted.

> The teacher used a variety of multicultural literature activities and encouraged students to express themselves through oral language and all forms of writing.

Vangchai's teacher used a variety of multicultural literature activities, and encouraged students to express themselves through oral language and all forms of writing. Vangchai thus became comfortable with sharing his feelings through journal writing. Moreover, as Vangchai wrote in his journal, he constructed meaning, strengthened his English competence, and gained confidence in himself as an important member of his class. Vangchai wants to become a lawyer and return to his homeland.

Immigrant children are challenged not only by cultural differences that exist between their native countries and the United States, but also by language differences. The next section provides more information about these learners.

Second Language and Bi-Dialectical Learners

Students of diverse linguistic backgrounds who use a language other than English for daily household communication, religious ceremonies, and celebrations are entering classrooms in unprecedented numbers (Faltis, 1997). Some of these children understand and speak little or no English. In 1993, the number of school-age children who lacked English proficiency and could not effectively participate in English-only classrooms was over 2.5 million. By the year 2000, this number is expected to be 3.5 million, and by 2020, to reach nearly 6 million (Faltis, 1997; Pallas, Natriello, & McDill, 1989).

Spanish-speaking children are the largest and fastest growing group of second language learners in the United States. This group includes populations of Mexican, Puerto Rican, Cuban, Central American, and South American origin. The Indo-Chinese and Asian country immigrant families (e.g. Chinese from Taiwan, Hong Kong, and more recently, Mainland China; Vietnamese; Hmong; Laotian; and Cambodian) compose the second largest population of school-age second language learners. These children, reared in homes in which only their native language is spoken by parents and caregivers, will understandably enter school with limited or no proficiency in English.

In Michigan, another sizable group of immigrants is composed of Arab students from the Middle East, most of whom speak Arabic and engage in Islamic religious practices. Significantly, southeastern Michigan has between 250,000 and 300,000 Arabic-speaking citizens—the largest concentration of such citizens outside of the Middle East (Faltis, 1997; Sarroub, 1999). In Dearborn schools, for example, 49% of the students speak Arabic, while 51% are non-Arabic-

Students of diverse linguistic backgrounds who use a language other than English for daily household communication, religious ceremonies, and celebrations are entering classrooms in unprecedented numbers.

speaking (Sarroub, 1999). This group of immigrants is often misunderstood and marginalized because many of its religious and lifestyle practices are unknown to most teachers.

Educational programs for second language learners focus on the target language only (English as a Second Language), or the development of students' fluency in both the home language and English (bilingual education). Tompkins (1997) argues that, based on what is known now about children's language development, programs for bilingual learners should be bilingual-bicultural in nature. These programs promote concept development in the home language *and* English, and include the culture and contributions of the native language to support the curriculum and the learner's self concept. Moreover, these programs build links between the community and the school, resulting in strong and successful experiences for the bilingual learner.

Mrs. Brown, a Venezuelan American, is a bilingual teacher for a population of students in Detroit which is primarily Spanish- and Arabic-speaking. She is so enthusiastic about her teaching that she refused a job as a Bilingual Coordinator, "a central-office job," because it would take her away from children. In her extremely successful "pull-out" program, she sees 90 children per week. Mrs. Brown uses a combination of students' experiences and language, and a print-rich environment. Her instruction also includes a systematic skills and decoding approach within the context of meaningful literature and texts.

The teacher uses a combination of students' experiences and language, and a print-rich environment. Her instruction also includes a systematic skills and decoding approach within the context of meaningful literature and texts.

Other students who speak a second language are those that use "Black English," a nonstandard dialect. According to Tompkins (1997), every speaker has an individual dialect, but some speak in a more standard dialect than others. Although Black English was once thought to be a haphazard and substandard language system, it is now recognized as a systematic and highly predictable form of language, with its own style, vocabulary, and grammar (Tompkins, 1997). Most speakers of Black English have acquired the language that is spoken in the home—the language of their parents and speech community, which shares interests, values, ambitions, and communication systems. Other groups, such as New Englanders, and people in Appalachian regions, similarly speak in nonstandard dialects. Even so, controversy surrounds the use and acceptance of Black English—whether to validate it, and how to implement literacy instruction for those who use it.

In a discussion of Black English, Janet,[2] a friend and veteran teacher, shared that she has "no part of that bad English in her classroom." She tells her students everyday, "Don't you come in here using that bad talk." She feels that as a black teacher, she owes it to her students to accept nothing but proper, standard English. "If they use a word like *ain't*, I immediately ask, 'What did you say!?' They quickly respond in the correct way" (personal communication, May, 1998). Janet is convinced that her approach is correct, feeling a strong responsibility to prepare her students to achieve academically and find employment. Her feelings are shared by many educators.

Variations among speakers of Black English exist, just as there are variations among speakers of other dialects. Some students are able to speak both Black English and standard English at will, based on the social setting and circumstances. For example, one morning I overheard my son, John, in a telephone conversation with one of his friends. It went something like this.

> "Hi Steve. How're you doing? You wanna play some basketball? OK! I'll call Marcus and tell him to come over to my house about 3:00. See ya!"

Variations among speakers of Black English exist, just as variations exist between speakers of other dialects. Some students are able to speak both Black English and standard English at will, based on the social setting and circumstances.

A few minutes later, I noted a similar conversation with a somewhat different dialect.

> "Yo Marcus! What's happening? Aw, I ain't doin' nothin' man. How 'bout some hoop? I just talked wi' Steve and he's game… about 3:00. Yo, man, at my pad. Later, man!"

He then hung up. Even had I not heard the names, I would have immediately recognized that Steve was white and Marcus was black. Many children possess John's code-switching ability. It was relatively easy for him to acquire standard English, the primary language of our home. The informal language (a form of Black English) used with Marcus was learned from his friends and used in less formal settings.

Teachers might expect that all children, whether they speak standard English or a dialect, have the ability to code switch. It is important that they not make negative judgments concerning students' language or academic competence based on their language use. On the other hand, it is critical that teachers provide systematic instruction to help students acquire standard English, underscored with sensitivity and respect for the students and their language.

> It is critical that teachers provide systematic instruction to help students acquire standard English, underscored with sensitivity and respect for students and their language.

Delpit (1995) equates the use of standard English with power, describing it as the power language, or the code of the culture of power. She suggests "that students must be taught the codes needed to participate fully in the mainstream of American life, not by being forced to attend to hollow, inane, decontextualized subskills, but rather within the context of meaningful communicative endeavors" (p. 45).

Children Who Are Poor

Children who live in poverty cut across all racial, cultural, and ethnic lines. These vulnerable students grow up, often with their single mothers, on the edges of society (Polakow, 1993). Although poor children are found most often in urban areas, the rural poor are increasingly prevalent in Michigan. These students sometimes live in shelters with grandparents or move from one relative to another. Their daily existence is often fraught with uncertainty and confusion, as they go to school hungry and face the realization that there may not be food when they get home. Polakow chronicles the story of Heather in her book *Lives on the Edge*, and poignantly reminds us of the children of the "other America":

> Seven year old Heather was easy to identify as a "problem" second grader as she sat at her desk pushed out in the hallway. The children passing by were not allowed to speak to her; neither was she allowed to speak to anyone. She could not go to recess, nor eat lunch with the others in the cafeteria anymore. [Her teacher said:] 'This child just does not know the difference between right and wrong—she absolutely does not belong in a normal classroom with normal children.' (Polakow, 1993, pp. 1–2)

As Heather walked to the office in her flimsy skirt, the teacher expressed her exasperation with the child, lamenting that "three times now we've caught her stealing free lunch and storing it in her desk to take home" (p. 2). Further questioning revealed that Heather, her mother, and her sister had such limited resources that their food stamps often ran out before the month was up. Heather had taken the extra lunch on three Fridays, knowing that there would be no other food until Monday when they would get their next free meals.

According to Polakow (1993), many experts have suggested that poor children require a structured, controlled instructional program in which order and compliance is encouraged. Brophy and Good (as cited in Polakow, 1993) have suggested:

> Low-[socioeconomic status]–low-achieving students need more control and structuring from their teachers:

Many experts have suggested that poor children require a structured, controlled instructional program in which order and compliance is encouraged. Others are critical of this "pedagogy of poverty," asserting that it precludes real teaching and learning.

more active instruction and feedback, more redundancy, and smaller steps with higher success rates. This will mean more review, drill, and practice, and thus more lower-level questions. (p. 149)

Haberman (1991), however, is critical of this "pedagogy of poverty," asserting that it precludes real teaching and learning. Haberman holds that good teaching occurs when teachers welcome difficult issues and events, and when they use human difference as a basis for the curriculum; design collaborative activities for heterogeneous groups; and help students apply ideas of fairness, equity, and justice to their world.

Good teachers reject a "pedagogy of poverty." Good teaching occurs when teachers welcome difficult issues and events, and use human differences as a basis for the curriculum.

Fortunately, some teachers embrace this type of pedagogy. Mrs. Mack is one such teacher. Although her children are not as desperately poor as Heather, some receive public assistance and have parents of meager means. Mrs. Mack offers her second-grade students a range of literacy encounters that extends their background knowledge. One specific project is a study of the states, evolving from a selection in their literature anthology. Mrs. Mack, realizing that most of her children had not traveled to different states, assigned them to write to all 50 state agencies, requesting postcards for all her students. They received post cards from every state. They proudly placed the postcards into small photo albums (purchased by Mrs. Mack, with each student contributing 10 cents), and subsequently wrote about and discussed each state's history, flower, motto, bird, and other pertinent information.

The students were totally engaged; developed word recognition skills; and learned to use reading, writing, oral language, and listening in a real and purposeful manner. In this classroom, Mrs. Mack values each child, and they, in turn, learn to value themselves. She takes strong exception to those who suggest that her students are incapable of "appropriate" social interactions or that learning must be limited to routinized drill and practice. The children in Mrs. Mack's room are happy and content in school. In fact, for many of them, it is the happiest and safest place they know.

Learners of Diverse Academic Abilities and Special Needs

Thus far, I have focused on students of diverse cultures, second language learners, immigrant students, and students who are poor. These students are most likely to be placed at risk and to find academic success elusive. However, as teachers plan and develop literacy instruction, they must consider the academic diversity among all students. Now more than ever, students with diverse academic abilities and physical and emotional needs populate our classrooms. These changes are due, to a great degree, to federal and state legislation that now requires public schools to provide a free and appropriate education for all students. This legislation further insists that the needs of these children be met, to the greatest extent possible, in regular classrooms.

Several principles can guide teachers as they work with students who are placed at risk because of poor academic achievement and special needs. First, all students are students with special needs, and literacy decisions should be made based on these needs. Second, traditional categorical designations (whether learning-disabled or gifted) used for legal or administrative purposes must never prevent teachers from providing students opportunities to develop their abilities to the fullest possible extent. Finally, having students with special needs in regular classrooms should be viewed as an opportunity for teachers and children

Traditional categorical designations (whether learning disabled or gifted) used for legal or administrative purposes must never prevent teachers from providing students opportunities to develop their abilities to the fullest possible extent.

to celebrate diversity and support each other in authentic learning communities.

Learners Who Experience Poor Academic Achievement

Children with exceptionalities lack the ability to attain their academic potential without special services, instructional materials, and/or facilities that extend beyond the requirements for the average child. These include students with specific learning disabilities, mental retardation, behavior disorders, language disorders, attention deficit disorder, speech and hearing impairment, or giftedness. Significantly, approximately 16–18% of school-age children fall into at least one of these categories (Hallahan & Kauffman, 1982; Learner, 1985; U.S. Department of Education, 1992). For many of these students, special education services are available. Increasingly, however, regular classroom teachers are expected to work with exceptional students within their classrooms (Leu & Kinzer,1998).

Students with learning disabilities represent 3.75% of all students between the ages of 6 and 21 (U.S. Department of Education, 1992). While these students are not a monolithic group—they exhibit a range of behaviors and characteristics—many experience some disruption in language processing. Because reading and writing are language-based processes, students with learning disabilities often have difficulty acquiring the strategies and skills necessary to read and write proficiently. Consequently, they fall behind, some more than two years below grade level (Harris & Sipay, 1990).

One student, David,[3] a third grader in a small town in mid-Michigan, was a student who was easily distracted and had a short attention span. Mr. Deckard, David's teacher, noted that David also possessed a wide store of knowledge about many topics. While observing David in a small literacy focus group, he became concerned about David's tendency to be distracted and his difficulty attending to the topic. Mr. Deckard was heartened by David's ability to contribute substantively to the discussion about the text, even when it appeared he was not listening. David's written assignments, however were almost illegible, and spelling was equally difficult for him, often precipitating frustration, agitation, and anxiety. Mr. Deckard made two decisions. The first was to make several adjustments within the regular classroom, including:

• limiting overstimulation in David's immediate learning environment;

• using functional reading experiences, building on David's interests;

• emphasizing oral language activities; and

• providing writing activities that allowed response at a level that was comfortable and appropriate (e.g., repetitive writing, patterned writing, short passages).

Mr. Deckard's second decision was to seek additional assistance from support professionals, including the school psychologist, social worker, and special education teacher. Mr. Deckard's insistence on working with David's strengths and identifying his needs allowed David to achieve a measure of success within his classroom.

Learners Who Experience High Academic Achievement

When we look at students of extremely high academic achievement, the term *gifted* often comes to mind. However, no one definition of gifted is universally accepted. Indeed, Gardner (Armstrong, 1994; Lazear, 1992) claims that there are seven or more forms of intelligence, including linguistic, logical-mathematical, spatial, bodily-kinesthetic, musical, interpersonal, and intrapersonal intelligence, and that individuals may be gifted in one or more of these areas. Given different definitions of giftedness, the prevalence of gifted students in the school-age population ranges from 2–20% (Turnbull, Turnbull, Shank, & Leal, 1995). These students generally demonstrate exceptional creativity, intelligence, motivation, artistic talent, verbal ability, and curiosity. Importantly, students with exceptional academic and creative abilities, like all students, need support and planned literacy activities in order to achieve at the level of which they are capable. If these students' needs are not appropriately addressed, many will hide their abilities, withdraw, act out, or exhibit behaviors that are incompatible with the expectations for students with exceptional ability.

> Students with exceptional academic and creative abilities need support and planned literacy activities in order to achieve at the level of which they are capable. If these students' needs are not appropriately addressed, many will hide their abilities, withdraw, act out, or exhibit behaviors that are incompatible with the expectations for students with exceptional ability.

Delisle (1987) asked students from throughout the United States how they felt about their exceptional abilities, schools, friends, families, and futures. For example, when asked "Are you gifted?" students replied:

> Girl, 8, Illinois: It depends on what you mean by gifted. I'm not what you would call brilliant, but I'm not dumb either. I do get some nice comments on my reading abilities, though. (p. 6)

> Boy, 8, Georgia: I am smart in some things, like football and dominoes, and unsmart in other subjects, like writing. (p. 6)

> Boy, 12, Connecticut: No, I'm not gifted.... I just think that my brain has been trained better than most. (p. 7)

> Girl, 10, Michigan: I believe I was born with a special gift but I don't believe I have quite found it yet. (p. 8)

> Some children who are gifted may downplay their abilities in order to "fit in," while others may realistically acknowledge and identify areas in which they are exceptional.

Significantly, some children who are gifted may downplay their abilities in order to "fit in," while others may realistically acknowledge and identify areas in which they are exceptional.

Some teachers find that an integrated curriculum in which students are actively engaged not only enhances learning but makes it exciting for all students, including the students of exceptional abilities. For example, Mrs. Harkema's fifth graders studied the northwest Indian nations during the 1850s (Diamond & Moore, 1995). They learned about their ceremonies; their rituals; their beliefs in the spirit of the eagle, beaver, and whale; and their reverence for the earth and all living things. Mrs. Harkema wanted her students to go beyond this basic knowledge, however, to comprehend how these values and beliefs influenced the Native Americans' reactions to the ordeals and dilemmas of this turbulent period. She used a recording of Chief Seattle's historic speech in which he eloquently lays out their choices—whether to relinquish their land to the white man in exchange for peace, or to continue to fight. The students, after thoughtfully discussing elements of the speech, were grouped into warriors, chiefs, hunters, and scouts from various tribes. They then reenacted the treaty meeting, offering arguments for and against the treaty signing. They engaged in serious and sometimes heated discussions before reaching their decisions, writing their parts and sharing them with the whole group. The chiefs and tribal members ultimately decided to sign the treaty.

This activity offered all students the opportunity to work in groups, with the academically gifted students challenging themselves and others to think critically and creatively about "real" issues and events. They used their listening, writing, oral language, and decision-making skills to discover solutions to a complex problem.

Concluding Comment

All of us, regardless of the students we teach, are learners as well as teachers. My undergraduate classes have now completed two-thirds of the semester. I have attempted to establish a learning community. I have certainly gotten to know each student as an individual, and, importantly, they have come to know and respect each other. We recently had lunch together at a Mexican restaurant in a section of town where half of the students go weekly for their school field placement. The lunch was initiated by several students, and the goal was twofold: to see more of the community, and to discuss the possibility of publishing some of their autobiographies.

As I have thought about the diverse group of learners in this chapter, I have continued to think about my class. I constantly wonder if they are learning the components of literacy needed to reach all of their students. Do they know enough about the use of literature in the literacy program? Do they have enough knowledge of onset and rimes, prefixes and suffixes, to help students decode words in meaningful contexts? Can they organize students into literacy focus groups and teach minilessons? But most of all, I wonder if they were able to get to know the students in their field-placement classrooms. If they are to successfully educate all children, preservice teachers must suspend judgment as they go into classrooms, leaving their stereotypes behind. They must listen to their students and get to know them. If they know their learners, they will necessarily develop a balanced approach to literacy, for they will have learned that no two learners have identical needs, nor do they learn in the same way. Delpit (1995, p. 183) quotes a "wonderful Native Alaskan educator: In order to teach you, I must know you." This is crucial for all teachers—that they know their students so that they can teach them more effectively.

Notes

1. All names are used with permission, unless otherwise noted.

2. Janet is a pseudonym.

3. Both David and Mr. Deckard are pseudonyms.

References

Adams, M. (1990). *Beginning to read: Thinking and learning about print.* Cambridge, MA: MIT Press.

Armstrong, T. (1994). *Multiple intelligences in the classroom.* Alexandria, VA: Association for Supervision and Curriculum Development.

Au, K. (1998). Social constructivism and the school literacy learning of students of diverse backgrounds. *Journal of Literacy Research, 30,* 297–319.

Calfee, R., & Piontkowski, D. (1981). The reading diary: Acquisition of decoding. *Reading Research Quarterly, 16,* 346–373.

Comer, J. P. (1984). Home-school relationships as they affect the academic success of children. *Education and Urban Society, 16,* 323–327.

Cushner, K., McClelland, A., & Safford, P. (1992). *Human diversity in education: An integrative approach.* New York: McGraw-Hill.

Delisle, R. (1987). *Gifted kids speak out.* Minneapolis: Free Spirit Publishing, Inc.

Delpit, L. (1988). The silenced dialogue: Power and pedagogy in educating other people's children. *Harvard Educational Review, 58,* 280–298.

Delpit, L. (1995). *Other people's children: Conflict in the classroom.* New York. The New York Press.

Diamond, B., & Moore, M. (1995). *Multicultural literacy: Mirroring the reality of the classroom.* New York: Longman.

Faltis, C. (1997) *Joinfostering: Adapting teaching for the multilingual classroom.* Columbus, OH: Merrill.

Haberman, M. (1991). The pedagogy of poverty versus good teaching. *Phi Delta Kappan, 73,* 290–294.

Hallahan, D. P., & Kauffman, J. M. (1982). *Exceptional children* (2nd ed.). New York: Prentice Hall.

Harris, A. J., & Sipay, E. R. (1990). *How to increase reading ability* (9th ed.). New York: Longman.

Heath, H. B. (1989). Oral and literate traditions among black Americans living in poverty. *American Psychologist, 14,* 367–373.

Hodgkinson, H. L. (1985). *All one system: Demographics of education—kindergarten through graduate school.* Washington, DC: Institute for Educational Leadership. (Eric Document No. ED 261101).

Littman, M. (Ed.). (1998). *A statistical portrait of the United States: Scoial conditions and trends.* Lanham, MD: Bernan Press.

Moll, L. (1989). Teaching second language students: A Vygotskian perspective. In D. H. Roen (Ed.), *Richness in writing: Empowering ESL students* (pp 55–69). New York: Longman.

Ladson-Billings, G. (1994). *The dreamkeepers: Successful teachers of African American children.* San Francisco: Jossey Bass, Inc.

Lazear, D. (1992). *Teaching for multiple intelligences.* Phi Delta Kappa.

Learner, J. (1985). *Learning disabilities: Theories, diagnosis, and teaching strategies* (4th ed.). Boston: Houghton Mifflin.

Leu, J., & Kinzer, C. K. (1998). *Effective literacy instruction.* Upper Saddle River, NJ: Merrill.

Manjarrez, C. A. (1991). Mis palabras. In D. Schoem (Ed.), *Inside separate worlds: Life stories of young blacks, Jews, and Latinos* (pp. 50–63). Ann Arbor: University of Michigan Press.

Neito, S. (1996). Lessons from students. *Harvard Educational Review, 64,* 450–473.

Pallas, A., Natriello, G., & McDill, E. (1989). The changing of the disadvantaged population: Current dimensions and future trends. *Educational Research, 18,* 16–22.

Pflaum, S. W., Walberg, H. J., Karegianes, M. L., & Rasher, S. P. (1980). Reading instruction: A quantitative analysis. *Educational Researcher, 9,* 12–18.

Polakow, V. (1993). *Lives on the edge: Single mothers and their children in the other America.* Chicago: University of Chicago Press.

Renzuilli, J. S. (1978). What makes giftedness? Re-examining a definition. *Phi Delta Kappan, 60* (3), 180–184, 261.

Sarroub, L. (1999). *Education: Arab American almanac.* Detroit, MI: UXL and Gale Research Limited.

Schieffelin, B., & Ochs, E. (1986). Language socialization. *Annual Review of Anthropology, 15,* 163–191.

Spiegel, D. L. (1998). Silver bullets, babies, and bath water: Literature response groups in a balanced literacy program. *The Reading Teacher, 52,* 114–124.

Tompkins, G. E. (1997). *Literacy for the 21st century: A balanced approach.* Columbus. OH: Merrill.

Turnbull, A. P., Turnbull, H. R., Shank, M., & Leal, D. (1995). *Exceptional lives: Special education in today's schools.* Upper Saddle River, NJ: Merrill.

U.S. Department of Education. (1992). *To assure the free, appropriate public education of all children with disabilities: Fourteenth annual report to Congress on the implementation of the Individuals With Disabilities Act.* Washington, DC: Author.

Wertsch, J. V. (1991). *Voices of the mind: A sociocultural approach to mediated action.* Cambridge, MA: Harvard University Press.

School-Family Connections: Why Are They So Difficult to Create?

4

Patricia A. Edwards, CIERA/Michigan State University

> Trying to educate children without the involvement of their family is like trying to play a basketball game without all the players on the court.
>
> (Bradley, cited by Olson, 1990, p. 17)

> Home-school partnership is no longer a luxury. There is an urgent need for schools to find ways to support the success of all our children.
>
> (Swap, 1993, p. 1)

> The crucial issue in successful learning is not home or school—teacher or student—but the relationship between them. Learning takes place where there is a productive learning relationship.
>
> (Seeley, 1985, p. 11)

> Shifting the blame for children's school problems from the school to the home is not a satisfactory solution. Mutual support is the answer.
>
> (Scott-Jones, 1988, p. 66)

Quotes are worth a thousand words! These reflect a dominant theme: Partnership is integral to the educational success of children and youth. These quotes also imply that academic outcomes will improve when parents and educators collaborate throughout students' educational careers. In the 1980s and 1990s, economic and social changes have caused both educators and parents to say, "We can't do it all" (Lewis 1991, p. 340). Rich (1987), of the Home and School Institute, contends that "families and teachers might wish that the school could do the job alone. But today's school needs families and today's families need the school. In many ways, their mutual need may be the greatest hope for change" (p. 62).

According to Berger (1991), "Home-school partnerships are an essential step forward" (p. 116). However, Berger is also quick to point out that "not everyone in the school will be comfortable with increased parent-school collaboration" (p. 116). Epstein (1986) reiterated this point by highlighting two conflicting theories. One encourages homes and schools to work together because they share the same goals for the students. The other theory argues that schools can achieve their goals to educate most efficiently when school and home remain separate, because the "professional status is in jeopardy if parents are involved in activities that are typically the teacher's responsibilities" (p. 227).

As we move into the next millennium, we know that Epstein's second theory doesn't work well. Rather, research and practice overwhelmingly support the need for and importance of home-school partnerships. Schools are particularly interested in connecting with families via parent involvement, as these two quotes illustrate:

> Parent involvement holds the greatest promise for meeting the needs of the child—it can be a reality rather than a professional dream. Of course, the bottom line is not only that involving parents holds the most realistic hope for individual children but also it serves as a hope for renewing the public's faith in education. This faith is needed if public schools are to continue as a strong institution in our democratic form of government, which, ironically, can only survive with a strong educational program. (Gordon, 1979, pp. 2–3)

Today's school needs families and today's families need the school. In many ways, their mutual need may be the greatest hope for change.

Parent involvement is on everyone's list of practices to make schools more effective, to help families create more positive learning environments, to reduce the risk of student failure, and to increase student success. (Epstein, 1987, p. 4)

Even though Ira Gordon and Joyce Epstein have highlighted the need for and importance of home-school connections and/or parent involvement, the fact that these partnerships remain "high rhetoric and low practice" has puzzled school administrators, teachers, and parents. Why aren't parents becoming more involved in schools? Are they to blame? Do schools play a role in low parent involvement? Do teachers? These are the issues that I address in the remainder of this chapter.

Parent involvement is on everyone's list of practices to make schools more effective. What has puzzled school administrators, teachers, and parents is why these partnerships remain high rhetoric and low practice.

Parent Involvement as School-Family Connection

It is easy for school administrators, teachers, and families to give reasons why school-family connections are tenuous and parent involvement in schools is low or even nonexistent. Some of the most common are:

• a history of distrust and miscommunication in family-school interactions;

• parents' sense of inadequacy and powerlessness in schools;

• the changing nature of parents' roles in children's lives;

• an unintentional exclusion of poor, minority, and/or immigrant parents from school activities.

These kinds of reasons point to a much broader, more critical issue: the struggle among researchers, teacher educators, and particularly school personnel to articulate their own definitions of parent involvement. Ascher (1987) points out that "parent involvement may easily mean quite different things to different people" (p. 1). She continues:

> It can mean advocacy: parents sitting on councils and committees, participating in the decisions and operation of schools. It can mean parents serving as classroom aides, accompanying a class on an outing or assisting teachers in a variety of other ways, either as volunteers or for wages. It can also conjure up images of teachers sending home notes to parents, or of parents working on bake sales and other projects that bring schools much needed support. Increasingly, parent involvement means parents initiating learning activities at home to improve their children's performance in school: reading to them, helping with homework, playing educational games, discussing current events, and so on. Sometimes, too, parent involvement is used most broadly to include all the ways in which home life socializes children for school. (p. 1)

Meanings of parent involvement are conveyed conceptually in Figure 9, which marks the way in which involvement is embedded in the interpretations, understandings, and personal meanings of the participants. This figure is intended to represent some of the phrases, comments, reflections, and statements that teachers, administrators, researchers, and policymakers have used when asked to define or describe parent involvement.

Henderson, Marburger, & Ooms (1986) share Ascher's contention that educators are not always clear what they mean when they talk about parent involvement:

> Most [educators] are probably referring to parents' participation in home-school activities—such as bake sales and fairs—to raise funds for the band uniforms or school computers, or they may mean parents helping in the classroom or on school trips. Some may be referring to special programs designed to encourage parents of young children to become more involved with their children in learning activities at home. Other educators feel less positive about parent involvement, thinking instead about incidents where parents have insisted that certain books be banned from the school library, particular courses not

School personnel have had difficulty establishing their own definitions of parent involvement from among its varied meanings, interpretations, and understandings.

Figure 9
Meaning-Centered Parent
Involvement

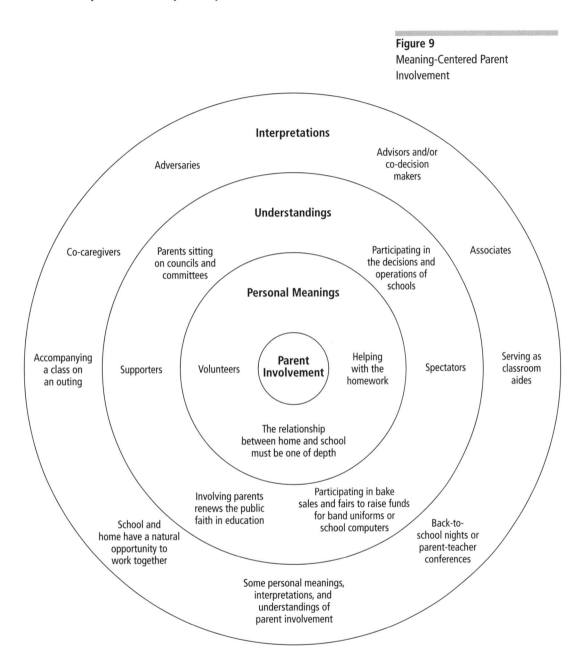

be taught, or a teacher be fired. Yet others are ambivalent about parent involvement, thinking about "Back-to-School" nights or parent-teacher conferences, which on some occasions turn out to be useful and constructive, but on others are boring rituals or even quite hostile encounters. (p. 2)

In order for schools and families to establish positive, effective partnerships, it is important for schools to ensure that the types of parent involvement initiatives they want are appropriate to the types of parent populations they serve.

In order for schools and families to establish positive, effective partnerships, it is important for schools to ensure that the types of parent involvement initiatives they want are appropriate to the types of parent populations they serve. If they do not take this into consideration, schools, parents, and communities will remain at odds with each other, which does not serve anyone well. Teachers must collaborate closely with parents and community members. In the long run all of the parties involved will reap the benefits.

What Do We Mean by Parent Involvement?

Research Definitions

In reviewing the literature, I discovered that **family involvement** has sometimes been used interchangeably with **parent involvement.** For example, in the descriptions of programs, researchers tended to flip-flop between the two terms in their discussions of the individuals involved in the program. What I found disturbing and surprising was that the researchers failed to document whether one parent, both parents, or the entire family were involved in and served by the program. The omission of this information adds to the confusion about the meaning of parent involvement.

Local Definitions of Parent Involvement Initiatives

I found that there are a number of other broad terms which have been used to describe family or parent involvement initiatives. Some of these are **business partnerships**, **home-school partnerships**, and **home-school-community partnerships.** These types of partnerships can be categorized as "local" because they consider how local community members can join with parents, teachers, and administrators to become more actively involved in family or parent involvement initiatives. This "team model" of schooling, which is the foundation for "Accelerated Schools" in California and those developed by Comer (1980), positions parent involvement as a powerful element, and strives to empower all parents rather than just a few parent volunteers (Seeley, 1989). In these partnerships, parent involvement is not a separate "project"; it is an integral part of the school's comprehensive plan to mobilize all available resources (e.g., parents, neighbors, community leaders) in an effort to help children achieve.

Local definitions of parent involvement are powerful because they make it possible to consider unusual or unique circumstances that require empathy and sensitivity. For example, the notion of **community organizations as family** is included in local definitions of parent involvement. Heath & McLaughlin (1991) explain this concept:

> Policy makers and practitioners concerned with American youth acknowledge the special and critical contribution of community organizations as resources that extend beyond family and schools. Their view recognizes the limitations of today's schools and families. Schools as social institutions are inadequate because they are built on outmoded assumptions about family and community. Too many families simply lack the emotional, financial, experiential, or cognitive supports that a developing youngster requires. Policy makers and practitioners no longer need to be convinced of the importance of positive local alternatives to a family- and school-based system of support. (p. 624)

As educators, we must be cognizant of the fact that "parents" can come in different forms. For many students, other people—grandparents, aunts and uncles, siblings, Big Brother/Big Sister organizations, and court-appointed guardians (i.e., foster parents)—act as parents, and they should be welcomed into and

Local definitions of parent involvement are powerful because they make it possible to consider unusual or unique circumstances. As educators, we must be cognizant of the fact that "parents" can come in different forms.

involved within the classroom as much as possible. The term *community organizations as family* further broadens the definition of "parent" to include community leaders and youth workers (i.e., Boys and Girls Clubs of America, Future Farmers of America) who are invested in the lives, dreams, and development of the children in their care.

Local definitions of parent involvement also consider parents' own educational needs and issues. These forms of parent involvement are typically embedded within a content area, and the underlying premise is that those parents' educational strengths and weaknesses greatly affect their children. For example, the definitions of **family literacy** and **intergenerational literacy** emerged from the idea that parents must be educated readers before they can become involved with their children's literacy development and academic lives. This idea is connected to adult education, specifically adult literacy, which provides programs to support parents' literacy development. This in turn will enable parents to become more proactive educators of their children (see Edwards, 1990, 1993).

Classroom Definitions of Parent Involvement

As educators, our definitions of parent involvement are particularly influential because we interact directly with our students and their families. Many teachers use a *delegation* model of parent involvement, where the types and forms of the involvement are teacher-directed. For example, many teachers request that parents chaperone their children and other students on field trips. Although the parent is technically "involved," the teachers has directed the interaction (e.g., telling parents to "keep your group together at all times") so that the parent has little or no input into the nature of the task. I suggest that teachers begin to use a *collaborative* model of parent involvement. Collaborative involvement will enable parents to support teachers and their instruction because teachers and parents talk about activities and set goals for the involvement together. Thus, the nature of the parent involvement is much more consistent than when the parent merely supervises field trips or bakes cookies for isolated occasions, and the nature of the involvement is more achievement-oriented. In collaborative parent involvement, parents have the opportunity to interact with students and teachers, so they can begin to learn the inner workings of the classroom.

> Collaborative involvement enables parents to support teachers and their instruction because teachers and parents can talk about activities and set goals together.

Collaborative parent involvement easily interfaces with more specific types of parent involvement that closely connect it to academic achievement. I provide here brief descriptions of these kinds of involvement in order to begin thinking about their impact on learning.

Participatory parent involvement (Potter, 1989), or **meaning-centered parent involvement,** emphasizes the roles that parents can play when they are involved in the classrooms, and it is important that these roles are meaning-centered. Parents are willing to become involved in schools, but they want their involvement to have a significant impact upon their children's achievement and educational experience. Some types of meaning-centered parent involvement are curriculum-centered. Teachers generally talk to parents using the curriculum as a foundation. Parents need to be aware of the school's goals and objectives, and how instruction meets these objectives, and teachers can discuss their curriculum in these terms with parents.

Other meaning-centered efforts are culture-specific. These programs are specifically designed for target groups of parents to encourage them to become involved in their child's educational achievement. For example, Raim (1980) developed a reading club for low-income Hispanic parents. Clegg (1973) provided low-income black parents with individually planned learning games in order to help them increase the reading achievement of their second-grade children. McConnell (1976) designed a bilingual multicultural education program for children of migrant and seasonal farm-workers. Gunther (1976) involved the families of prekindergarten children in an English as a Second Language program. The families were selected for the program on the basis of family background and their children's inability to speak English due to their recent arrival in the United States. Shuck, Ulsh, and Platt (1983) encouraged low-socioeconomic-status parents in a large inner-city school district to tutor their children using Parents Encourage Pupils (PEP) calendar books and individualized homework activities tallied in progress charts. The results indicated that the parent-tutoring program had a significant impact on the improvement of children's reading scores.

A third meaning-centered form of parental involvement is developmentally based. This is one of the most critical ways that parents can become involved in their children's academic success. There needs to be a scope and sequence of activities centered around the curriculum at each grade level that helps parents to understand what kinds of things they can do at home to support their children's literacy development. This helps parents to understand how to be involved and provides a structure for their involvement.

There needs to be a scope and sequence of activities centered around the curriculum at each grade level that helps parents to understand what kinds of things they can do to support their children's development.

Rethinking Parent Involvement

As you can see, there are many factors to consider in establishing a definition of parent involvement. First, who are the parents and what roles should they assume? Second, what kinds of involvement are advantageous for our school? Finally, what terms should be used to accurately portray the kind of balanced parent involvement we want? From the many conversations I have had with school staffs in different parts of the United States, I have come to find that once entire school communities or individual classroom teachers begin to think seriously about parent involvement, they tend to think about it using the four-step process illustrated in Figure 10.

Stage One
Developing Definitions
Stage Two
Deciding on Types
Stage Three
Examining Perceptions
Stage Four
Implementing Practices

Figure 10
Stages of Thinking About Parent Involvement

These stages can be illustrated in terms of the questions asked to guide the process of improving parent involvement programs. These questions occur at both the school and classroom levels.

School-Level Questions

Over the years, many schools have puzzled over questions such as

• Should teachers and administrators formulate a singular/multiple definition(s) of parent involvement, which represents the school's philosophy of parent involvement?

• Should schools develop specific policies about the roles parents may or should assume?

These kinds of questions are important for administrators to consider in that they set school policy. Principals and other school administrators might organize family nights or other types of events, but is very important that these officials have thought about deeper and broader definitions of parent involvement. Further, schools have puzzled over a question raised by Berger (1983):

> Does the thought that parents could be involved as education policy makers in conjunction with the school interest or threaten you? (p. 1)

This question is very important because it acknowledges that school administrators can view more parent involvement as a blessing or a curse. Schools have also puzzled over questions like the ones posed by Greenwood & Hickman (1991):

• What types of parent involvement have the strongest impact on different types of student achievement (e.g., higher order and lower order)?

• What types of parent involvement have the strongest effects on parent and student attitudes and behaviors?

• What parent and family characteristics influence student performance and parent involvement?

• What types of parent involvement work best with different socioeconomic statuses and ethnic families? (p. 287)

Classroom-Level Questions

In addition to these school level questions, many teachers have puzzled over questions that directly impact their individual practices of parent involvement:

- What should I do? How can I do more in my school/classroom to promote meaningful parent involvement?
- How should I reorganize my classroom instruction based on what I know about my students' home situations and their parents' ability to help them?
- What do I need to know so I won't offend parents, particularly parents of minority students?
- How should I interact with parents who have an ideology of parent involvement that conflicts with my own expectations?
- Should I only expect the parents of my students to be involved in their education? When the parents of my students choose not to be involved, should I seek out other family or community members to serve as advocates for these children?
- Should I began to think about parent involvement initiatives in terms of my students' social, emotional, physical, and academic environment? Are my expectations for parent involvement unrealistic based on the families of the children I teach?
- How can I begin to rethink, in my school/classroom, the taken-for-granted, institutionally-sanctioned means for teachers and parents to communicate (e.g., Parent Teacher Association meetings, open house rituals at the beginning of the school year, letters and telephone calls to parents, etc.)?

All of these questions reflect various stages in individual teachers' thinking about parent involvement, and these questions are an important part of the process of conceptualizing and understanding parent involvement. Furthermore, these questions help teachers target the kinds of parent involvement they need for their classrooms. Teachers can ask these questions to begin generating specific ideas for parent involvement. More importantly, these questions can and should be included in staff development work-

Many teachers have puzzled over questions that directly impact their individual practices of parent involvement. How can I do more in my school/classroom to promote meaningful parent involvement? How should I interact with parents who have an ideology of parent involvement that conflicts with my own expectations?

shops to challenge teachers to reflect on the wide range of questions that need to be addressed when considering parent involvement initiatives.

Models for Thinking About Parent Involvement

There are three models that can help school administrators and teachers transform their thoughts about parent involvement into a framework for action. These models will help school personnel organize pertinent information about students, their families, and their communities that will inform strategies for increasing parent involvement.

First, Bronfenbrenner (1979) describes the ecological environment in terms of four macrostructure levels. Since the school is a microcosm of society, he is reminding educators that there are social "forces" affecting children and their development. Level 1 is the child's immediate, primary settings (e.g., home, school); level 2 is the interaction between immediate settings; level 3 involves settings beyond the child (e.g., parents' jobs); and level 4 includes a wide range of developmental influences, such as war or national economic crisis, which produce subcultures.

> The Demographic Parent Profile is a short questionnaire that compiles information about the school's surrounding community.

Second, the Demographic Parent Profile is a short questionnaire that compiles information about the school's surrounding communities (see Edwards, in press). A sample list of questions on the profile is provided below:

• What is the predominant socioeconomic status of the neighborhood?

• In what conditions are the homes around the neighborhood? Are they mostly apartments, single-family homes, or a mix?

• What racial or ethnic groups are represented in the neighborhood? Which is the majority group?

- What age groups are represented in the neighborhood? Which is the majority group?

- Where are the public libraries located? Stop at the library and find out if there is a local newspaper, and if there is, skim it. Also, find out if there is a local history you might read.

- Count the number of churches. What religions do they represent? Where are they concentrated?

- What is the economic base of the community? What industries are here? What commercial enterprises? What is the community's level of economic health?

- What services does the community provide for children?

- Where are the "hangouts"?

- How would you characterize the "tone" of the community? Optimistic? Busy? Depressed? Orderly? Unruly? Quiet?

- What other characteristics of this community stand out for you?

These questions are critical to understanding some of the community-level issues that might affect parent involvement.

Third, Henderson, Marburger, and Ooms (1986) offer a means for constructing a "Profile of Parent Involvement in Your School." In this model (see Figure 11), Henderson et al. (1986) define the participatory roles that parents can play in the school. For example, some parents act as partners, while others are supporters, or simply "audience members." It is extremely important for teachers and administrators to think about what types of roles parents play in order to construct the kinds of involvement needed in the classroom and/or school.

Some parents act as partners, while others are supporters or simply "audience members." It is extremely important for teachers and administrators to think about what types of roles parents play.

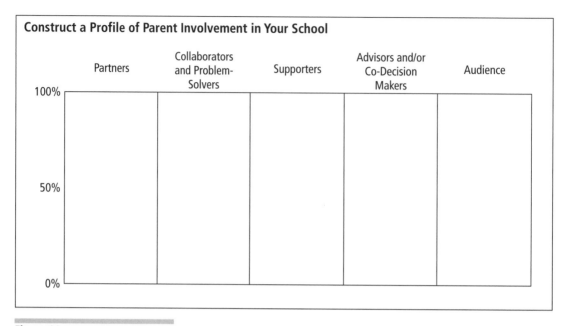

Figure 11
Parent Involvement Profile

Concluding Comment

As you can see, multiple definitions and varied personal meanings, interpretations, and understandings of parent involvement have emerged from teachers, administrators, and policymakers. You've seen the variety of roles parents may assume, and the beliefs about parent involvement that influence individual definitions, perceptions, and practices. Further, you've learned the school and classroom level questions that must be asked when thinking about parent involvement, and several stages and models of thinking about the issue.

As teachers and administrators, you will see the payoff if you think about involvement as I have outlined it in this chapter. If you as teachers are convinced to "buy in," administrators will then provide the support.

References

Ascher, C. (1987). *Improving the school-home connection for poor and minority urban students.* New York: Teacher College Institute for Urban and Minority Education.

Berger, E. H. (1991). *Parents as partners in education: The school and home working together.* Columbus, OH: Charles E. Merrill.

Berger, E. H. (1983). *Beyond the classroom: Parents as partners in education.* St. Louis, MO: The C. V. Mosby Company.

Bronfenbrenner, U. (1979). *The ecology of human development.* Cambridge, MA: Harvard University Press.

Clegg, B. E. (1973). The effectiveness of learning games used by economically disadvantaged parents to increase the reading achievement of their children. Paper presented at the annual meeting of the American Education Research Association, San Francisco.

Comer, J. P. (1980). *School power.* New York: The Free Press.

Edwards, P. A. (1990). *Talking your way to literacy: A program to help nonreading parents prepare their children for reading.* Chicago: Children's Press.

Edwards, P. A. (1993). *Parents as partners in reading: A family literacy training program* (2nd ed.). Chicago: Children's Press.

Edwards, P. A. (in press). *Rethinking parental involvement in multiple contexts: Concepts and case studies of real teachers and parents, real struggles and efforts.* Needham, MA: Allyn & Bacon.

Epstein, J. L. (1987). Parent involvement: State education agencies should lead the way. *Community Education Journal, 14* (4), 4–10.

Epstein, J. L. (1986). Parents' reactions to teacher practices of parent involvement. *Elementary School Journal, 86,* 277–293.

Gordon, I. J. (1979). Parent education: A position paper. In W. G. Hill, P. Fox, & C. D. Jones (Eds.), *Families and schools: Implementing parent education* (Report No. 121) (pp. 1–5). Denver, CO: Education Commission of the States.

Greenwood, G., & Hickman, C. (1991). Research and practice in parent involvement: Implications for teacher education. *The Elementary School Journal, 91* (3), 279–288.

Gunther, P. E. (1976). *Basic skills after-school prekindergarten program, 1975–1976*. Brooklyn, NY: New York City Board of Education, Office of Educational Evaluation. (ERIC Document Reproduction Service, No. ED 141-476).

Heath, S. H., & McLaughlin, M. W. (1991). Community organizations as family. *Phi Delta Kappan, 72* (8), 623–627.

Henderson, A., Marburger, C. L., & Ooms, T. (1986). *Beyond the bake sale: An educator's guide to working with parents*. Columbia, MD: National Committee for Citizens in Education.

Lewis, A. C. (1991). Coordinating services: Do we have the will? *Phi Delta Kappan, 72* (5), 340.

McConnell, B. (1976). *Bilingual mini-school tutoring project. A state of Washington URRD (Urban, Rural, Racial, Disadvantaged) Program. Final Evaluation, 1975–76 Program Year*. Olympia, WA: Washington Office of the State Superintendent of Public Instruction. (ERIC Document Reproduction Service No. 135–508).

Olson, L. (April, 1990). Parents as partners: Redefining the social contract between parents and schools [Special issue]. *Education Week, 9* (28), 17–24.

Potter, G. (1989). Parent participation in the language arts program. *Language Arts, 66* (1), 21–28.

Raim, J. (1980). Who learns when parents teach their children? *The Reading Teacher, 34*, 152–155.

Rich, D. (1987). *Schools and families: Issues and actions*. Washington, DC: National Education Association.

Scott-Jones, D. (1988). Families as educators. *Educational Horizons, 66*, 66–69.

Seeley, D. S. (1989). A new paradigm for parent involvement. *Educational Leadership, 47* (2), 46–48.

Seeley, D. (1985). *Education through partnership*. Washington, DC: American Enterprise Institute for Public Policy Research.

Shuck, A., Ulsh, F., & Platt, J. S. (1983). Parents encourage pupils (PEP): An inner-city parent involvement reading project. *The Reading Teacher, 36*, 524–529.

Swap, S. M. (1993). *Developing home-school partnerships: From concepts to practice*. New York: Teachers College Press.

5

A Michigan Early Literacy Parent/Teacher Collaboration

Deanna Birdyshaw, Michigan Department of Education

This chapter describes what we at the Michigan State Department of Education believe to be a success story in collaborative work among parents, teacher educators, teachers, and state department members toward improving early literacy instruction for the students in our state. I am chairperson of the Early Literacy Committee, based in the State Department of Education, and I serve as a liaison in some ways between the State Department and the Michigan Reading Association. In this chapter, I first describe how the Early Literacy Committee came to be, and particularly, how it emerged as a strong collaborative organization. (See Figure 12 for a chronology of these events.) Second, I describe how the members of the committee used discussion and collaboration on specific projects to enhance early literacy instruction within our state. Third, I highlight what we learned through our experience. I end with implications, which I present in terms of our "next steps."

As English Language Arts Consultant for the Michigan State Department of Education, my responsibilities include developing state content standards and benchmarks for grades K–12 and participating in the development of state assessments (Michigan English Language Arts Standards).[1] I am also expected to organize and conduct professional development activities that provide guidance in implementing instruction that is aligned with state standards and assessments. Because a major focus of my role is to inform educators and parents about state initiatives and literacy programs, the majority of my time is spent working with teachers and teacher educators in state department committees and conferences.

Michigan has made a strong commitment to providing learners with the best possible learning environment. This commitment includes developing a curriculum framework that identifies rigorous standards for content, instruction, assessment, and professional development. Michigan's goal of ensuring that all children read well and independently by the

Figure 12
Early Literacy Commitee Chronology

February 12, 1996	Steering Committee meets to plan goals of ELC
April 2, 1996	First meeting of ELC committee occurs
January 1997	Pamphlet "What Do Parents Want To Know About Early Literacy Programs?" is published
February 1, 1997	First ELC parent/teacher collaborative conference on balanced early literacy instruction takes place
April 5, 1997	Second ELC parent/teacher collaborative conference on balanced early literacy instruction takes place
January 1998	Governor Engler announces goals for the Reading Plan for Michigan
March 16, 1998	Michigan Reading Association Annual Conference Parents Day—a full day of presentations designed to inform parents about balanced early literacy instruction—is held
August 1998	READY (readiness kits for parents of infants, toddlers, and preschoolers) is published
October 9 & 10, 1998	Third ELC parent/teacher collaborative conference on balanced early literacy instruction, expanded to include early childhood component, takes place
December 1998	The *Michigan Literacy Progress Profile* and *Reading and Writing Portfolio* are published

end of third grade is taken seriously and supported with the resources for designing and implementing high-quality educational programs to obtain this goal. In Michigan, the State Department enjoys close, collaborative relationships with teacher organizations, university staff, and community organizations. Michigan's educational initiatives often begin as grassroots efforts disseminated with the assistance of professional organizations such as the Michigan Reading Association, the Michigan Council of Teachers of English, the Michigan Association for the Education of Young Children, and the Michigan Education Association. We at the State Department have been committed to maintaining this focus, even as the national scene has become more complicated, and at times, even divisive (Levine, 1994).

Like many parents around the country, Michigan parents read articles in local newspapers and national magazines challenging the value of instruction based on a whole language philosophy (Levine, 1994). They looked with interest upon the findings of a special educational task force established to investigate California's declining performance on the National Assessment of Educational Progress (California Reading Task Force, 1995). Some members of Michigan's State Board of Education began to advocate exploration of educational programs that employed direct instruction of phonics.

In the context of these events, the Michigan State Department of Education received a call from a parent in 1996 who wanted to know what the State Department was doing about phonics instruction. Her call was eventually directed to me, since one of my duties is to keep parents informed about state language arts policies. The parent had two young children whom she had taught to read using an intensive phonics program before they entered school. She felt

We are fortunate in Michigan that the state department enjoys close, collaborative relationships with community and teacher organizations and university staff.

a responsibility to ensure that tax dollars were used to support programs that included direct instruction of phonics. Since we were in the process of developing state language arts standards, she wanted to know how they addressed phonics. Further, she wanted the standards to be of a level of specificity to ensure that all children received intensive phonics instruction. This parent was influential in her community's politics, representing a group of parents who were very active in their community's schools. She and her peers followed national debates on "reading wars" and felt well-informed about issues related to direct instruction of phonics, invented spelling, and use of context clues in word recognition strategies.

My conversation with her raised issues that the State Department of Education would need to address. Michigan has a tradition of supporting local control in curriculum matters, while providing guidance through high standards established by the State Board of Education. The Early Literacy Committee and state department curriculum consultants wanted to maintain a local district focus on helping children achieve high levels of literacy, and wanted to avoid setting English Language Arts (ELA) standards that narrowed the focus to direct instruction of basic skills. The parent's views were shared by several State Board of Education members who advocated a traditional curriculum emphasizing intensive early phonics instruction. In 1995, when the Board of Education members were asked to approve the ELA standards, there was a long and sometimes heated discussion over whether or not the standards contained sufficient reference to basic skills such as spelling, phonics, and grammar. The standards were eventually approved, but Board members asked that the benchmarks that would be written to further explicate the ELA standards make clear reference to phonics, spelling, and grammar.

My conversation with the parent was also significant because it occurred during the time that the State Board of Education was asked to receive the newly written benchmarks. Several Board members were still concerned about the level of specificity in the ELA standards and wanted the benchmarks to emphasize student behaviors consistent with a traditional curriculum. They invited consultants from other states to address the Board of Education at their October 24, 1997, meeting and to provide arguments for revising the benchmarks to reflect direct instruction of basic skills. Bonnie Grossen of the National Center to Improve the Tools of Education addressed the State Board of Education and discussed the importance of incorporating performance objectives based on the intensive teaching of phonics into the benchmarks. A videotape of students being instructed using the Direct Instructional System in Arithmetic and Reading (DISTAR) program was shown to reinforce Grossen's comments. Despite this presentation, the benchmarks, which focus on the integration of reading, writing, speaking, listening, viewing, and representation in authentic performances of literacy, were formally received by the Board. According to some reviewers, the state standards and benchmarks were rigorous standards describing high expectations for student learning, but they did not provide sufficient specificity to ensure that "basic skills" (i.e., intensive phonics training) would take their rightful place in primary level classrooms (Glidden, 1998; Stotsky, 1997). This conversation indicated to me that it was imperative that we find a way to inform parents about the research upon which the standards and benchmarks are based and to help them understand the importance of achieving high levels of literacy application in addition to developing basic reading and writing skills.

How We Got Started

Although conversations across interest groups within Michigan were not as controversial as they seemed to be in other states, we still felt the tension as different agendas from various groups came into conflict. We were concerned that the stage had been set for policy decisions that might restrict teacher and local district decision making in matters related to early literacy curriculum. I decided to invite the parent mentioned above to meet with me. I also invited a teacher from a large urban district in southeast Michigan. Our goal was to discuss how we might establish a forum for parents and teachers to discuss their views on early literacy instruction and formulate common ground on which to build agreement.

The first meeting was tense, but civil. It seemed to illustrate Edwards' point (this volume) that while educators may value parents' contributions, when parents become involved in educational policy, educators may view parents as threatening their autonomy. Such tensions played out in our first meeting. The parent began by citing several stories that illustrated her view: Teachers lacked sensitivity to parents' concerns and continued to use whole language strategies that had she felt had obviously been shown to be ineffective. She said that she represented a large and growing group of parents who were tired of being dismissed and were dedicated to changing curriculum to reflect a stronger emphasis on basics, especially phonics. The parent brought copies of publications supporting her opinion (e.g., California Reading Task Force, 1995; Adams, 1990). She showed us a copy of a letter from learning specialists who supported her

The first meeting with the concerned parent was tense, but civil. It seemed to illustrate Edwards' point (this volume) that, while educators may value parents' contributions, when parents become involved in educational policy, educators may view parents as threatening their autonomy.

position (Pesetsky & McLivoid, 1995). The teacher responded by describing strategies incorporating letter-sound concepts into broader teaching strategies (Clay, 1991; Cunningham, 1995). She noted that most teachers believed in and practiced a balanced approach to early literacy and cited cases in which parents and teachers worked as partners in helping children to develop early literacy skills.

While no one actually argued, after each presented their opinion, there was little agreement. Furthermore, neither parent nor teacher seemed optimistic that differences in perceptions would ever be resolved. However, the parent, the teacher, and I did agree that we must do something to bring these different perspectives together for the good of the children in our care. We decided to create a committee to discuss issues associated with early literacy instruction, consisting of an equal number of parents, teachers, and teacher educators. I agreed to publicize the effort, and ask for volunteers. We planned to meet monthly for the remainder of the 1996 calendar year.

> We decided to create a committee to discuss issues associated with early literacy instruction. The committee would consist of an equal number of parents, teachers, and teacher educators.

By the first meeting we were able to gather approximately five parents, four teacher educators, and five teachers. Some of the parents were avid supporters of direct instruction (e.g., DISTAR, Orton Gillingham), and some favored constructivist approaches to learning such as those reflecting more of a learner-centered philosophy of instruction (Goodman, 1986) and Reading Recovery (Clay, 1993). Teachers all described themselves as advocating a balanced approach to learning; teacher educators working in university and college settings varied in their views, but generally assumed a centrist position.

The committee became known as the Early Literacy Committee (ELC), and we began our first meeting by shaping our goal. It was—and still is—to establish a forum where parents, teachers, and teacher educators can discuss early literacy issues with the purpose of establishing a common ground upon which we can all agree. Committee members wanted to create an open dialogue in which everyone was free to express his or her opinion. The first and most important issue agreed upon was that each of the committee members wanted all children to learn to read and write well. With this as the foundation, committee members began a long series of discussions in which diverse viewpoints were shared and supported (McIntyre & Pressley, 1995). It took several meetings to attain the level of trust and respect we needed in order to become a productive committee.

What We Did

The committee needed a focus, so we decided we would create a useful product for parents. Committee members decided to create a flip chart that answered questions parents frequently asked about early literacy programs:

- What should I see in a quality early literacy program?
- Where does phonics fit in an early literacy program?
- Why should my child learn to read and write at the same time?
- What is invented spelling, and why does my child use it?
- What behaviors will I see as my child learns to read and write?
- What can I do to help my child become a better reader and writer?
- How can I work with the teacher to ensure the success of my child?

The ELC formed small groups with a representative number of parents, teachers, and teacher educators to respond to the questions.

When a group finished a draft response, they met with the entire committee for review. Working closely in small groups allowed parents and teachers to form a clearer understanding of each other's views and to learn to appreciate the concern and dedication each had for helping children attain high levels of literacy. Small groups seemed to be able to resolve philosophical differences and incorporate each person's opinion into the response. However, when the response was brought to the whole group, it became necessary to clarify and refine the responses to meet the broader understandings of the larger group. Each statement and position was carefully and rigorously scrutinized, and a subtle change began to occur. Parents began to use language such as, "I understand what we're saying here, but I don't think some of my friends will. We will need to accommodate this perspective." Parents might then describe a narrower view of literacy acquisition than they, themselves, currently espoused. Teachers did the same thing. A teacher might say that a certain response could alienate a group of educators because it did not take a favored philosophy into account. The teacher might personally understand why the response was worded as it was, but would suggest that writers find a way to assure teachers that the response would not exclude other teaching strategies. ELC members were beginning to understand each other and to consider and respond to alternate points of view. In the end, the writing process brought us closer to the common ground we sought. Each time committee members revised the text of the flip chart to include a wider variety of perspectives, we clarified our group's understanding of what we meant by the term **balanced instruction.**

> Working closely in small groups allowed parents and teachers to form a clearer understanding of each other's views.

The committee published the flip chart, *What Do Parents Want To Know About Early Literacy Programs?* (Michigan Department of Education Early Literacy Committee, 1997). The Michigan Reading Association agreed to print and distribute the flip charts to state educators and parents.

With the successful completion of the flip chart work, committee members wanted other parents, teachers, and teacher educators to have a similar experience. The committee decided to hold a conference, using the launch of the flip charts as the reason. The Michigan Reading Association supported the committee, providing the funds to organize the conference. Committee members felt strongly that the conference should represent the collaborative nature of the ELC, so the conference was publicized as a conference *by* teachers and parents *for* teachers and parents. The committee decided to present a session on each of the flip chart questions. Parents and teachers teamed to prepare presentations incorporating both parent and educator perspectives.

The Michigan Department of Education publicized the conference by sending notices to schools and asking them to send pairs of teachers and parents to the conference. Advertisements explained that attendance at the conference would give parents and teachers an opportunity to discuss major issues related to early literacy and provide them with a knowledge base from which to continue their discussions after the conference. Registration for the January 1997 conference exceeded expectations and was closed, so a second conference was planned for later that year. Both conferences were overwhelming successes, generating requests to repeat them at various sites throughout the state.

Because of the clear parent interest, the Michigan Reading Association asked the ELC to create a "Par-

Committee members felt strongly that a conference should represent the collaborative nature of the Early Literacy Committee, so the conference was publicized as a conference by teachers and parents for teachers and parents.

ent's Day" at their annual state conference, beginning with the March 1998 event. The committee organized a day that featured presentations on quality early literacy instruction, integrating phonemic awareness and phonology into a balanced literacy program, assessing early learning, and strategies for parents and teachers to work together to ensure that all children achieve high standards of literacy. ELC members brought in samples of children's work to decorate the room, along with posters of enlarged pictures of children engaged in a variety of learning experiences. A lowered registration fee was established for parents, and special flyers were sent to parent organizations throughout the state. Parents' Day was a huge success; over 300 people attended each of the sessions. Parents and teachers praised the sessions and the opportunity to share a common experience that could become the foundation for continuing conversations.

To extend the collaboration that had developed between the ELC and itself, the Michigan Reading Assocation asked the ELC to create a series of parent/teacher discussion kits. These kits are being designed to be used at parent-teacher organization meetings, curriculum nights, and other events where parents and teachers gather to talk about early literacy instruction. There will be four kits. One will describe a balanced early literacy program, a second will discuss early literacy assessment, a third will demonstrate how parents and teachers can support each other in providing experiences that develop literacy skills in young children, and the fourth will discuss early literacy research. Each kit will contain a videotape that illustrates major issues associated with each topic. Whenever possible, clips of children, teachers, and parents interacting in literacy environments will be featured. Each kit will contain focus questions designed to facilitate discussion, an article or two addressing the topic, and a resource list for further exploration.

In January 1998, Michigan's Governor John Engler announced that the state would develop a reading plan that would include four components:

• readiness kits designed to help parents of infants, toddlers, and preschoolers prepare their children for learning to read and write;

• a diagnostic, prescriptive reading assessment process;

• a reading progress portfolio; and

• a model summer school program.

The ELC was given the task of developing a progress portfolio and an early literacy assessment notebook for students in preschool through third grade (Michigan Department of Education Early Literacy Committee, 1998). Study groups composed of teachers and parents were formed to explore best practices in assessing early literacy development. Early Childhood specialists joined the committee so that a seamless continuum could be developed between preschool educational programs and early elementary programs.

The assessment notebook that resulted is a compilation of eleven assessment tools which are linked to instructional strategies for teachers and parents.

The assessment notebook we created includes 11 assessment tools linked to instructional strategies for teachers and parents. The assessments reflect a framework that lays out benchmark assessments to measure student growth in writing, reading fluency, oral language, comprehension, and attitudes about learning. Teachers are encouraged to take stock of these assessment areas on a regular basis. Additional assessments in the notebook measure more specific skills such as letter/sound knowledge, concepts of print, phonemic awareness, and sight vocabulary. Teachers are encouraged to use these assessments to "dig deeper" when children do not seem to be making adequate progress in major assessment areas. The notebook is accompanied by a portfolio, which is designed to travel with the child from preschool through third grade. It contains a record sheet that summarizes the information gathered by teachers and caregivers describing an individual child's literacy growth along a developmental continuum.

The assessment notebook further represents the collaborative relationships nurtured by the ELC. The philosophy of the notebook emphasizes that the purpose of early literacy assessment is neither to weigh nor measure children; it is to help children grow in their literacy skills. For that reason, each assessment task is designed to provide teachers and parents with information to help them make informed decisions about what each child needs to advance his or her literacy. The connection between assessment and instruction needs to be seamless. Tools used to learn about literacy progress need to be shared with parents so that they can join in the effort to provide their children with an environment that enriches their children's literacy experiences.

> The purpose of early literacy assessment is neither to weigh nor measure children; it is to help children grow in their literacy skills.

What We Learned

The lessons learned by members of the ELC were reciprocal—educators learned from parents, and parents from educators. Our experiences with one another promoted mutual respect and increased our understanding of how to improve the learning opportunities of our young children. The lessons we learned fell into five areas: (a) we have more in common than we had originally thought; (b) we need each other; (c) we can make a difference through partnerships with interested parties; (d) we need a broader understanding of research; and (e) our public messages must be broad, reflecting balance among positions.

There Is Common Ground After All

We discovered that we shared an overriding concern for children and for their learning success. This shared concern provided a rudder to steer us through the rough waters we encountered on our way toward establishing a strong collaborative relationship. The concern we share for children, therefore, became the foundation for all of the other lessons we learned.

We Need Each Other

We learned that we need each other. Reaching the goal of giving all children the learning opportunities they need to achieve high levels of literacy depends on creating collaborative relationships based on trust and respect for the views of others. The State Department of Education cannot influence educational practice without first gathering the grassroots support of educators, parents, and teacher educators. For example, the parents learned more about why teachers make the decisions they do in classrooms, and were exposed to a body of knowledge related to teaching literacy that they, as parents, may not have considered. The educators learned about parents' perceptions of literacy and the basis of these parents' concerns. The committee learned that the best way to maintain teacher support is through powerful professional organizations such as the Michigan Reading Association and the Michigan Association for the Education of Young Children. We need each other, but we also must understand each others' needs.

Partnerships Are Crucial for Developing Strong Frameworks

Partnerships through collaborative activities allow us to develop the best approaches to teaching our students. We learned from the partnerships established among members of the ELC, and realized that these should carry over into the broader community. For example, we believe an important way to make a difference in teachers' practices is to develop a partnership with teacher educators who design and implement preservice and graduate teacher training programs. We believe that to provide children with quality learning experiences, we must build a strong, supportive relationship with their parents. We also believe that to build a quality early literacy program, we must form a network of knowledgeable collaborators who can formulate a philosophy for early literacy instruction based on good research and best practice.

Given these beliefs about the importance of partnerships, we learned to look closely at what might interfere with their development. We learned to make sure that all committee members' voices could be heard and that their constituencies were accurately represented. When beliefs clashed, we recognized that we needed to get to the bottom of the differences. For example, the issue of whole language instruction was also associated with student choice and learning centers. To some parents, this evoked images of unruly classrooms in which their children were not given the structure that they needed to feel safe and learn. The same practice that encouraged some students to take learning risks and expanded their learning opportunities overwhelmed children who were used to structured environments, and caused them to withdraw from learning experiences. When teachers talked about classrooms, they talked about creating environments in which all children could receive the instruction they need to achieve high standards of literacy. Often, when parents talked, they focused on their own child. We had to keep reminding ourselves that we were creating opportunities for all students.

We believe the best way to build a quality early literacy program is to form a network of knowledgeable collaborators who can formulate a philosophy for early literacy instruction based on good research and best practice.

We learned that if we believed strongly enough in the perspective we wanted placed into our description of a balanced early literacy program, we had to find a way to convince others. Sometimes we postponed completing our discussion until a later meeting to provide time to gather more supporting evidence and restructure our arguments (Allington & Woodside-Jiron, 1997; Grossen, 1997; Hiebert et al., 1998; Lemann, 1997; Pearson, 1996; Snow, Burns, & Griffin, 1998; Wingert & Kantrowitz, 1997). We found that with additional time to reflect, we sometimes ended up accepting others' positions while maintaining the integrity of our own philosophies.

Committee members also learned that in collaborative enterprise, extreme positions carry little weight. We learned that it was best if we drew on our beliefs, no matter how extreme they might be, but worked to shape a centrist position to better serve our students. This meant that we had to maintain a balance among constituencies and perspectives in each of our meetings, and recognize that, if these were out of balance, we must postpone final decisions. Further, if there were extreme differences, we learned to probe deeply into what created those differences. This caused us to note that what we sometimes took for simple truths were far more complex (e.g., "simply teach more phonics" or "simply read to your children more"). What we learned is that there are no simple answers if we want to improve literacy instruction for *all* students.

We Need a Better Understanding of Research

As a result of the questions that arose in our collaborative meetings, we learned that we needed to broaden our understanding of research.

As a result of the questions that arose in our collaborative meetings, we learned that we needed to broaden our understanding of research. Sometimes we would state a conclusion and provide support from research and then have someone in the group offer some research that refuted our conclusion. It appeared that most of us occasionally selected our evidence from journals and organizations that supported only our perspective. In our own way, we began to understand the importance of looking for converging research. As the individuals in our group became more comfortable with each other, they began to state their arguments and support with more objectivity and less passion. This allowed us to arrive at our own conclusions and further develop the common ground we had established.

Public Messages Must Be Broad and Balanced

We learned that we must provide interested parties with a broad and balanced message. The best defense against becoming the victim of extreme points of view is to educate parents, teachers, and administrators so they understand content addressed at school and strategies used to ensure that all children progress in their literacy development. For example, we believe that teachers should talk to parents about spelling development and explain the progressive stage through which children learn to demonstrate their knowledge of spelling in their writing. By predicting for parents the stages through which their child will progress, we prepare these parents for the changes that they will see in their child's writing. Throughout the year, as parents observe predicted stages, they can be confident in the teacher's knowledge of literacy acquisition, and can potentially support the strategies used at school by providing the child with similar learning opportunities at home.

The best defense against becoming the victim of extreme points of view is the education of parents, teachers, and administrators.

In summary, the committee's goal was to facilitate dialogue. Committee members believed we had reached a level of understanding that made it possible for us to find common ground upon which to discuss educational issues; we wanted to share this understanding with others. Most of all, the committee wanted to build a strong community of parents and teachers who could resist the influence of extreme points of view that mixed political and social issues with educational issues. We wanted to create a forum where parents and teachers could address any and all educational topics that aroused concern or conflict.

Where Do We Go From Here?

The ELC's work continues today. The Reading Plan for Michigan has provided committee members with tools to expand the dialogue among parents and teachers. Subcommittees of parents and teachers are working diligently to find ways to help parents of infants, toddlers, and preschoolers increase their awareness of the role they play in preparing their young children to be learners. Subcommittees of the ELC are developing a training program designed to prepare teachers to use the *Michigan Literacy Progress Profile* and the *Michigan Reading and Writing Portfolio* to make informed instructional decisions for the individual children in their classrooms and to create partnerships with each child's parents. Some ELC members are working with legislators to help them design and implement policy which supports a balanced approach to early literacy and provides resources for parent programs and professional development for teachers.

Members of the ELC are working with the Michigan State Department of Education to revise standards for teacher education to include more instruction in the area of early literacy. Efforts are being made to strengthen collaborative relationships among educational organizations such as the Michigan Reading Association, Michigan Association for the Education of Young Children, Michigan Council of the Teachers of English, and the Michigan Association for Supervision and Curriculum. A plan is being formulated to hold a national conference which brings together teachers, teacher educators, researchers, policymakers, parents, and professional organizations to continue developing a plan for assuring that all children learn to read well and independently. The work of the committee continues, the momentum is growing, and committee members' beliefs in the power of their collaboration provides confidence that supports working on bigger and more far-reaching challenges.

Concluding Comment

Thanks to the interest of one concerned parent, the Michigan Early Literacy Committee was formed. Begun as a modest endeavor, the committee now provides a forum for examining our divergent views about literacy education. The views come from a wide spectrum of individuals who represent a variety of roles, communities, and cultures. The work of the ELC continues with its monthly meetings, its conference presentations, and the projects it supports.

Begun as a modest endeavor, the ELC now provides a forum for examining our divergent views about literacy education.

If we are to avoid being swept along with the educational pendulum that moves us periodically from one extreme to another, we must communicate clearly with one another. We must place the focus on what really counts for all of us—the learning of children. We have found in Michigan that collaboration across professional communities and parents has given us the base we need to explore educational issues, gain needed support, and strengthen our early literacy programs.

If we are to avoid being swept along with the educational pendulum that moves us periodically from one extreme to another, we must communicate clearly with one another.

Notes

1. Michigan's English Language Arts standards were developed by teachers and teacher educators as part of a federally funded project entitled the Michigan English Language Arts Framework (MELAF). In August 1993, the Michigan Department of Education and the University of Michigan were awarded a three-year grant from the U.S. Department of Education to develop and disseminate a K–12 English language arts curriculum framework. Ten integrated language arts standards were developed with accompanying benchmarks written for grade level clusters: early elementary, later elementary, middle school, and high school. The ten standards, along with two additional standards written by State Board of Education members, were approved by the Michigan State Board of Education in July 1995. The standards address the following areas of an integrated English language arts curriculum: meaning and communication, language, literature, voice, skills and processes, genre and craft of language, depth of understanding, ideas in action, inquiry and research, and critical standards. The standards and benchmarks are designed to guide the development and implementation of an English language arts curriculum at the local district level. (Michigan Department of Education, 1996).

References

Adams, M. J. (1990). *Beginning to read: Thinking and learning about print.* Cambridge, MA: MIT Press.

Allington, R. I., & Woodside-Jiron, H. (1997). *Thirty years of research on reading: Adequacy and use of a "research summary" in shaping educational policy.* Albany, NY: National Research Center on English Learning and Achievement.

California Reading Task Force. (1995). *Every child a reader.* Sacramento: California Department of Education.

Clay, M. M. (1991). *Becoming literate: The construction of inner control.* Portsmouth, NH: Heinemann.

Clay, M. M. (1993). *Reading Recovery: A guidebook for teachers in training.* Portsmouth, NH: Heinemann.

Cunningham, P. M. (1995). *Phonics they use: Words for reading and writing.* New York: Harper Collins College Publishers.

Glidden, H. (Ed.). (1998). *Making standards matter: 1998.* Washington, DC: American Federation of Teachers.

Goodman, K. (1986). *What's whole in whole language?* New York: Scholastic.

Grossen, B. (1997). *Thirty years of research: What we know about how children learn to read—a synthesis of research on reading from the National Institute of Child Health and Development.* Santa Cruz, CA: Center for the Future of Teaching and Learning.

Hiebert, E. H., Pearson, P. D., Taylor, B. M., Richardson, V.. & Paris, S. G. (1998). *Every child a reader: Applying reading research in the classroom.* Ann Arbor: CIERA/University of Michigan.

Lemann, N. (November, 1997). The reading wars. *Atlantic Monthly, 280* (5), 128–134.

Levine, A (1994). The great debate revisited. *Atlantic Monthly, 274* (6), 38–44.

McIntyre, E., & Pressley, M. (1995). *Balanced instruction: Strategies and skills in whole language.* Norwood, MA: Christopher-Gordon Publishers.

Michigan Department of Education. (1996). *Michigan curriculum framework.* Lansing, MI: Author.

Michigan Department of Education Early Literacy Committee. (1998). *Michigan literacy progress profile.* Lansing, MI: Michigan Department of Education.

Michigan Department of Education Early Literacy Committee. (1997). *What do parents want to know about early literacy programs?* Grand Rapids, MI: Michigan Reading Association.

Pearson, P. D. (1996). Reclaiming the center. In M. F. Graves, P. van den Broeck, & B. M. Taylor (Eds.), *The first R: Every child's right to read.* New York: Teachers College Press.

Pesetsky, D., & McLivoid, J. (July, 1995). A letter from forty Massachusetts specialists in linguistics and psycholinguistics addressed to Dr. Robert V. Antonucci, Commissioner of Education, Commonwealth of Massachusetts.

Snow, C. E., Burns, M. S., & Griffin, P. (Eds.). (1998). *Preventing reading difficulties in young children.* Washington, DC: National Research Council.

Stotsky, S. (Ed.). (1997). *State English standards.* Washington, DC: Fordham Foundation.

Wingert, P., & Kantrowitz, B. (October 27, 1997). Why Andy couldn't read. *Newsweek,* 56–64.

6

A Balanced Early Literacy Curriculum: An Ecological Perspective

W. Dorsey Hammond, Oakland University

As we move into the new millennium, it is appropriate that we as educators pause to take stock of how we support the literacy development of young children. The debate of how best to teach young children to read and write has been a part of our legacy for an entire century. Literally thousands of articles, books, and monographs have been written on the subject. Particular books have served to heighten the debate, from *Why Johnny Can't Read* (Flesch, 1955) and *Learning to Read—The Great Debate* (Chall, 1967), to *Becoming A Nation of Readers* (Anderson et al., 1985) and the more recent *Beginning to Read* (Adams, 1990a).

Among the many issues discussed over the last four decades are the nature of the process, the nature of the learner, the complementary nature of learning to read and learning to write, and appropriate teaching methodologies. Two specific issues within this context have very much defined the debate: (a) the role of phonics in learning to read, and (b) the types of text and related materials used to teach children to read.

Literacy in an Historical Perspective

Since the 1950s, the phonics pendulum has swung between one extreme of equating learning phonics with learning to read and the other extreme of seeing phonics as a minor contributor to reading acquisition. The text type issue has ranged from advocating word- or vocabulary-controlled readers (e.g., Look, look, see Sally, see Sally run), to experimenting with linguistic or grapheme-phoneme control (e.g., The fat cat sat, the cat ran), to augmenting or changing the alphabet, to sentence patterning or predictable books such as *Brown Bear, Brown Bear, What Do You See?* (Martin, 1963). In some cases, one of these text types was the primary medium through which children learned to read. In other cases, different text types were used in various combinations. Each approach and each text type made particular assumptions about the process of learning to read.

It is difficult to trace trends in literacy instruction historically, for they have never represented a singular movement. For example, during the middle to late 1980s and early 1990s, when whole language was very much in vogue, there remained pockets of intensive phonics instruction, sometimes represented by a single teacher, a specific school or district, or a community of districts. Conversely, in the decade of the 1970s, when the vast majority of school districts used vocabulary-controlled basal readers, one could find teachers rejecting these methods and materials and teaching children to read using experience charts, library books, and writing with invented spellings. Despite this caveat, the pendulum swings can be described in the following manner. Beginning in the 1960s, our field has seen a concentrated effort to determine the most effective ways of teaching beginning reading with the twenty-seven federally-funded

It is difficult to trace trends in literacy instruction historically, for they have never represented a singular movement.

first-grade studies (see Barone, 1997). These studies were relatively inconclusive when analyzed as a whole, though individual studies provided important findings and conclusions. For example, one of the first-grade studies (Stauffer & Hammond, 1969) initiated a study of the effects of early writing with invented spellings on learning to read (see also Barone, 1997).

Jeanne Chall, in *Learning to Read: The Great Debate* (1967), signaled—with her strong recommendation of code emphasis approaches—a greater emphasis on *breaking the code* programs. Intensive phonics programs became more popular, as did the practice of breaking reading into its smallest components for instructional purposes. The period from 1968 through 1975 was also a time in which teaching by specific objectives was promoted.

However, disenchantment with these approaches began to move the literacy pendulum back toward the center beginning in the mid 1970s. The late 1970s and early 1980s saw a renewed emphasis on reading comprehension, much of which can be attributed to the work at the Center for the Study of Reading at the University of Illinois at Urbana-Champaign, under the direction of Richard C. Anderson.

Concurrently, there was an increased awareness of writing as a legitimate part of early literacy development (see Graves, 1983), and more attention was paid to the use of authentic children's literature and language-patterned and predictable books to teach young children to read. It was during this period in the 1980s that the whole language movement became popular in primary-grade classrooms.

Despite the major contributions of the whole language movement to the literacy process, this movement appears to have suffered from two unfortunate occurrences. Because of its child-centered focus, many teachers, school districts, and even entire states embraced whole language without understanding its underlying philosophy or the instructional strategies it encompassed. For example, it was not uncommon to talk to classroom teachers across the country who equated whole language with whole class teaching. Other teachers viewed whole language as primarily *not* using a basal reading program. Still others viewed whole language as teaching exclusively with novels or chapter books. For some teachers whole language meant not having to teach skills anymore. None of these views captured the essence of the whole language movement.

The second occurrence was that some whole language advocates appeared to have become too extreme by implying or directly stating that phonics instruction and word study simply weren't important and that direct teacher instruction might actually impede the natural literacy development of young children. These two factors—a lack of understanding of whole language by many who claimed to be using a whole language curriculum, and a reluctance of a select few whole language advocates to endorse phonics, word study, or focused teacher instruction—created a context for change.

The tide began to turn again with the publication of Marilyn Adams' (1990a) book, *Beginning to Read*. Adams advocated a very strong focus on phonemic awareness and phonics in the earliest stages of reading. She rejected the importance of such methodologies as using predictable books and experience charts as major contributors to learning to read (Adams, 1990b). This position on early literacy learning is having a significant effect on the profession today. Thus, our field has seen profound pendulum swings to the educational right, to the educational left, and back again over the past three decades. This trend continues today, and as we enter the 21st century, the debate continues within the profession between the many segments of the literacy community.

There is risk in characterizing our recent history in this manner. Clearly, one person's extremism is another's centrist position, and vice versa. There is little doubt, however, that there have historically been distinctly different emphases in literacy instruction and in our beliefs about how children learn to read. Some states and regions have been more immune to drastic shifts than others. Both California and Texas, two of our most populous states, seem to have been particularly susceptible to extreme changes in their views about literacy. One has only to examine the Texas Literacy Frameworks, respectively, of the late 1980s (see for example Texas Reading Proclamation, 1988) and their Literacy Frameworks of the middle to late 1990s (see for example Texas Reading Initiative, 1997) to note striking changes in the orientation, philosophy, and psychology of learning to read. Certainly we can disagree about which approach within these Frameworks is more appropriate, but it is difficult to ignore the dramatic differences that arise in just a few years. What was in vogue in 1988–89 is unacceptable today, and ideas viewed as enlightened positions in 1998–99 were wholly unacceptable just 8–10 years ago.

A continuing dialogue and debate is healthy in any profession, but these extreme swings should cause the profession considerable concern. Some classroom teachers appear to be confused about what to believe and how best to teach reading. School and instructional leaders have been disadvantaged by an inability to build long term consistency and consensus among teaching staffs, to say nothing of the tremendous financial costs of procuring the newest materials and staff development consistent with the

> There is little doubt that there have been distinctly different emphases in the latter half of this century on literacy instruction and in our beliefs about how children learn to read.

latest trends. Students have sometimes been disadvantaged by getting inconsistent instruction through the grades as they encounter teachers with widely divergent views of how to teach children to read and write. As a profession, we have been disadvantaged by appearing to the larger community of parents, business people, and professionals as though we don't know what we are doing (Levine, 1994). The teaching profession has been disadvantaged by the substantial energy used up in this debate on beginning reading when there are other literacy issues that desperately need our attention.

What the Debate Is About

The first issue is whether learning to read is basically a linear process of learning, of focusing on one aspect of reading before moving on to another, or whether in learning to read several behaviors should occur simultaneously.

There are many issues that divide the literacy profession, ranging from the nature of the reading process and our theories about how individuals learn to the nature of the learners themselves. Four major issues on early literacy instruction illustrate the deep divisions within the profession. The first is whether learning to read is basically a linear process of learning, of focusing on one aspect of reading before moving on to another, or whether in learning to read several behaviors can occur simultaneously. Adams (1990a) appears to take the former position, asserting that phonemic awareness occurs first, then phonic instruction, which is basic. Later, she maintains, one can focus on comprehension. In contrast, Wells (1986), Holdaway (1979), Routman (1988), Weaver (1994) and others would argue for a more comprehensive approach to literacy instruction which would address not only phonics and word study but extensive reading, writing, and attention to comprehension from the very beginning. These contrasting views appear to be incompatible. Whichever position one adopts will in large measure define the context and character of one's early literacy program.

A second issue that is basic to the debate is the role of context in early reading, specifically the role of context on word recognition and word processing. Adams (1990), Perfetti & Zhang (1996) and Lyon (1998) represent a view that context effects are minimal in learning to read, even in the early stages of the process. For example, Perfetti (1997), referring to early reading instruction, writes, "It is misleading to focus… on such side issues as context, comprehension, or even getting meaning from print…. These commonly cited goals are not the heart of what learning to read is all about" (pp. 56–57).

In a recent article, Lyon (1998) points out that research has demonstrated that context has little effect on word and text processing. However, a reading of the original Gough et al. (1981) research referred to by Lyon indicates that their subjects were adult and college students who were skilled readers, not five-, six-, and seven-year-olds at the early stages of literacy. Moreover, Gough et al. looked at context at the single phrase or sentence level, not connected discourse. The limitations of the Gough et al. study in terms of adult subjects and the reading materials used is indeed sobering. It raises an important question about whether one can generalize about the reading behaviors of young children from research done on adult subjects.

Interestingly, it is difficult to persuade practicing teachers that context does not facilitate word recognition and word processing, given their extensive experience seeing the facilitating effects. This suggests a contrast between some researchers and teachers working with students. The context issue is central because it defines both theory and practice. How we address the context issue dramatically

It is difficult to persuade practicing teachers that context does not facilitate work recognition and word processing, given their extensive experience of seeing the facilitating effects of context.

affects the strategies used in the classroom, the types of materials used, and the assessment procedures implemented. Those who argue for context effects suggest that readers' background experiences or schemata and their intuitive knowledge about language facilitate text and word-level processing even at the earliest stages. In this view, meaning is not only the goal of reading; it is also one of the means or processes by which readers actually learn to read. In other words, reading for meaning even in the earliest stages makes learning to read easier. The division is particularly strong on the context effects issue.

A third issue that divides our profession is the extent to which reading is a natural or unnatural act. Lyon (1998) argues that learning to read is unnatural. Goodman (1992), on the other hand, argues that reading is very much a natural act. Again, we see strongly divergent views. Instead of engaging in a debate about whether learning to read is or is not a natural act, perhaps we'd do better to ask, "To what extent can we make learning to read more of a natural act through curriculum design and instructional strategies?" Is it possible to engage young readers in literacy learning experiences that seem natural or less arbitrary to the learner? Literacy activities such as experience stories, in which students share experiences that teachers record in the natural language of the learners and then encourage children to read their own ideas in their language patterns, certainly appear to promote reading as a natural process. Allowing children to write their own stories and express their ideas through invented spelling seems natural to most anyone who spends time observing language-rich and meaning-based first-grade classrooms. Moreover, it is natural for young children to read predictable texts, using repetitive language patterns and pictures to support the early reading process. It is natural for

> Instead of engaging in a debate about whether learning to read is or is not a natural act, perhaps we'd do better to ask, "To what extent can we make learning to read more of a natural act through curriculum design and instructional strategies?"

young readers to use pictures to help give them a sense of what the text is about. It is also natural for young children entering school to want to learn to read. That desire, motivation, and excitement should not be squandered in the early days and months of school.

Not all parts of learning to read are natural. The code itself, particularly many letter-sound correspondences, is arbitrary and indeed confusing to the young learner. If, therefore, the vast portion of early reading centers around this arbitrary and unnatural code, then children are likely to experience learning to read as an unnatural act. If, however, one capitalizes on the child's experiences, the language facility and the predisposition to make meaning, as Wells (1986) has demonstrated, then reading seems more natural to the young learner. This is another important reason to advocate a multidimensional and balanced approach to literacy learning.

The fourth major issue that defines our view of early literacy is the concept of **automaticity**— namely, that word recognition must be accurate, rapid and require little conscious attention so that attention can be directed to the comprehension process. Indeed, the concept of automaticity, as articulated by LaBerge and Samuels (1974), is a helpful one. One reason students may not comprehend text is that they are spending all of their energy and attention on *figuring out the words*. The remedy by some reading authorities is to spend more time on word study until word recognition becomes automatic. However, the road to automaticity must be more than a focus on phonics or decoding. One approach is through word study. But other approaches are effective, such as providing students with text that is familiar and predictable. Also, it is likely that extensive early writing with invented or approximate spelling helps establish and automatize phoneme-grapheme relationships, thus contributing indirectly to automaticity in reading. Samuels (1979) recognized the efficacy of repeated reading strategies in promoting automaticity. Thus, very early in the learning-to-read process, attention should be paid to fluency with a variety of instructional activities.

Another issue that is raised with the concept of automaticity is the implication that once automaticity is reached, comprehension will naturally or likely follow. Many experienced teachers in primary, intermediate, and middle schools make this assumption erroneously. Many teachers can cite examples of students who are fluent and automatic (i.e., sound good when they read aloud) but fail to construct meaning and comprehend text. There may be a variety of reasons why this happens. It is possible is that our young students are not receiving enough instruction in effective comprehension strategies, or are being asked to read texts that are not potentially meaningful. Another plausible explanation for the numbers of students who can decode but fail to construct meaning and comprehend text is that learning to read in the early stages may not have been seen by learners as an act of constructing meaning. If children spend the majority of their time in the early grades focusing primarily on phonics activities, learning about individual letter sounds or words, and are consistently urged to *sound it out* when reading text, their view of what reading is may be skewed.

> One plausible explanation for the numbers of students who can decode but fail to construct meaning and comprehend text is that, in the early stages, these students may not have seen learning to read as an act of constructing meaning.

In summary, one's stand on these four issues—(a) the foundations of the learning-to-read process, (b) the effects or noneffects of context, (c) the extent to which educators can make learning to read natural, and (d) the concept of automaticity—determines how one structures the literacy curriculum for young learners.

Why Balanced Literacy Instruction Is Important

Balance in early literacy instruction is important for several reasons. Studies have shown that a balanced literacy curriculum produces the best results. This was demonstrated in our early studies in first and second grade (Stauffer & Hammond, 1969; Stauffer, 1970), as well as in our recent work with two elementary schools in Ferndale, Michigan, between 1994 and 1997. In thirty years of working closely with primary-grade teachers in many schools and several cultures, I have concluded that a balanced curriculum produces more and better readers over both the short and long term. Highly effective primary grade teachers balance instruction from the earliest days of school by engaging young children in meaningful text through the use of experience charts and predictable books. They engage children in writing on a daily basis. They teach phonics and word study in both a focused and informal manner. They provide many opportunities for repetition through shared reading, choral reading, and repeated reading activities. They talk with children about stories and ideas and words in a language- and print-rich environment. These are the teachers who, year after year, seem to produce outstanding literacy performances from their young students.

Highly effective primary-grade teachers balance instruction from the earliest days of school.

It should not surprise us that a balanced curriculum is so essential, because reading is a multidimensional process. Anderson et al.'s *Becoming a Nation of Readers* (1985) describes skilled readers as constructive, strategic, fluent, motivated, and lifelong. As we read, we use our prior knowledge, decipher print, access word meanings, interpret, evaluate, reflect, anticipate—all in a relatively rapid manner. Some behaviors are dependent upon other behaviors. Reading is a multifaceted process, and learning to read has

Learning to read does not lend itself to a series of small incremental steps presented in a linear fashion. If reading is a multifaceted process, it makes sense that its instruction be multifaceted as well.

been likened to learning to ride a bicycle, in that several actions and behaviors occur simultaneously or recursively. Learning to read does not lend itself to a series of small incremental steps presented in a linear fashion. If reading is a multifaceted process, it makes sense that its instruction be multifaceted as well.

Another reason balance is so important is that it capitalizes on the nature of the learner. Unfortunately, this factor may not be taken into account sufficiently when building a model for early literacy. Young children bring a wealth of competencies and behaviors to the learning-to-read equation. As Wells (1986) points out, children by kindergarten age are quite competent in language usage. They usually exhibit the basic grammatical sentence patterns of mature speech—an amazing feat in four or five short years. In addition, young children are naturally curious and have a drive or desire to make sense of their world and the activities in which they are engaged. There is solid empirical evidence that young children are skilled meaning-makers.

Therefore, there are two implications for curriculum specialists in recognizing the nature of the learners. First, children want to engage in reading and literacy activities that result in meaning making—reading stories, asking questions about stories, and interpreting text and pictures, as well as writing personal and meaningful messages. From the very beginning, the content of reading activities needs, in large measure, to be meaning-based. Second, young children need to see that the classroom activities and lessons in which they are engaging are leading to something meaningful. In other words, when learners begin to wonder why they are doing a certain task, their commitment and energy begin to wane.

A balanced curriculum can address these issues by building on the natural language and meaning-making ability of the learner. Those literacy activities that are less meaningful to the child are better learned in the context of a balanced curriculum. For those of us who work in and observe primary classrooms, there is little doubt that capitalizing on the learners' strengths produces results in achievement as well as an attitude, energy, and work ethic which have a significant impact on literacy development.

The idea of balance is not a new one. Heilman (1993) cautions us about imbalance when he writes:

> To make reasonable progress, the beginning reader must acquire three closely related skills.
>
> • Mastering and applying letter-sound relationships
>
> • Enlarging sight vocabulary
>
> • Profiting from context clues while reading
>
> Beginning reading instruction is so important because it is here that children develop a sense of what reading is. It is not good instruction to devote the first few months of reading to one of the above skills while ignoring the other two. This kind of approach will confuse a child regarding the true nature of the reading process.... Early instruction should help learners develop the insight that these three skills complement each other in helping to crack the two codes—word identification and meaning. The only way children can miss the fact that reading is a meaning-making process is to receive instruction that masks this fact. (pp. 24–25)

These are wise words indeed. In fact, Heilman, who arguably has written the most popular and enduring books on phonics, deems balance so important that he has cautioned his literacy colleagues about this issue in each of the nine editions of his book, written between 1963 and 1999.

In summary, the case for balance is a strong one. Balanced literacy curricula recognize the multifaceted behavior of learning to read. Balanced curricula capitalize on the nature of the learner as a language user who has a predisposition to make sense of his or

The case for balance is a strong one. Balanced literacy curricula recognize the multifaceted behavior of learning to read, and capitalize on the nature of the learner as a language user who has a predisposition to make sense of his or her world.

her world. Balanced curricula produce in young readers the idea that reading is about making sense and constructing meaning, an insight that will serve them well as they move through the intermediate and upper grades.

Balanced Literacy—A View Into the Classroom

Balance can be viewed from various perspectives. One perspective that is particularly helpful is that of a primary classroom of young learners. The central question is, what kinds of activities and learning experiences would a teacher and a classroom of first-grade students engage in over several school days? A related question focuses not only on the *what*, but on the *why*. Within the context of an early literacy classroom, there is one dominant and limiting factor—instructional time.

Therefore, one must construct a curriculum where instructional time is finite. In any classroom, teachers have to set priorities about what will be taught, when it will be taught, and how it will be taught. Figure 13 includes a combination of instructional experiences, all designed to promote growth in literacy. The elements are shown in a circle and represent what one might reasonably see occurring in a typical primary school classroom. The divisions between the components are fluid and modifiable.

The literacy experiences depicted in Figure 13 are highly interrelated. Included in this illustration are activities that address language development, word recognition, fluency, comprehension, writing, exposure to literature, and the development of concepts about how young readers need to think about reading and writing through metacognitive activities. In some activities, the child works under direct teacher guid-

One must construct a curriculum where instructional time is finite. In any classroom, teachers have to set priorities about what will be taught, when it will be taught, and how it will be taught.

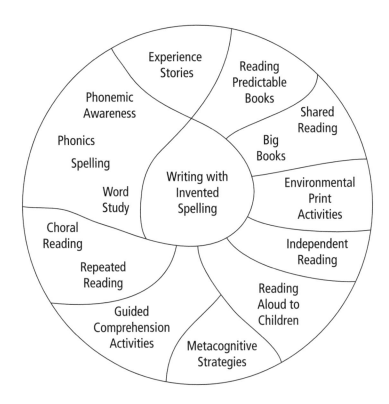

Figure 13
A Balanced Literacy Curriculum

ance in small groups; in other instances, the young learners work cooperatively with peers. On other occasions, the learner works independently under indirect teacher guidance. This is a picture of a well-organized classroom fostering a high level of interest and energy.

The circle represents the constant—instructional time. Therefore, if a teacher chooses to increase the amount of time on any one activity, he or she must reduce the time designated for some other activity. To a limited degree, of course, such tradeoffs are acceptable and may even be encouraged. However, there is a point where the tradeoffs may be so excessive that they become detrimental. Once the instructional experiences are significantly out of balance, literacy development is likely impeded.

I believe five points are relevant to understanding this figure of the Balanced Literacy Curriculum. First,

If a teacher chooses to increase the amount of time on any one activity, he/she must reduce the time designated for some other activity.

Experience Stories

- Engages child in the process of reading at the earliest stages
- Engages child in language and meaning construction
- Develops concept of story and of word
- Develops concepts of print and the ability to track print
- Develops core of known words
- Develops and reinforces sound-symbol correspondences
- Addresses fluency at early stages
- Models the writing process
- Is aesthetically attractive to young readers

Writing (with Invented/Temporary) Spelling

- Engages learner in meaning construction
- Signals the communicative powers of language
- Develops and reinforces sound-symbol correspondence
- Provides practice in conventions of print, including punctuation, capitalization, etc.
- Provides insights into the reading process
- Engages learners in personal and independent writing

Predictable Texts

- Engages learner in act of reading at earliest stages
- Develops and reinforces a core of known words
- Develops and reinforces letter-sound correspondence
- Facilitates tracking of print
- Addresses fluency at early stages
- Facilitates prediction of language and story content
- Is aesthetically pleasing to young learners

Choral/Repeated Reading

- Allows young readers to read at early stages in supportive situation
- Develops fluency
- Develops new and reinforces known words
- Develops confidence in the emergent reader

Phonemic Awareness/Phonics/Word Study

- Establishes sound discrimination
- Establishes knowledge of letter-sound correspondences for reading
- Facilitates writing with invented spelling
- Allows child to move from a known to an unknown word
- Aids in fluency
- Helps promote independence in word recognition

Figure 14
Components of the Learning-to-Read Process

the circle does not represent one day in a first- or second-grade classroom. However, over the course of several days, all or nearly all of these instructional components should be observed. Second, the instructional mix within the circle is different for different masterful teachers. Third, the mix changes relatively significantly through the kindergarten, first-, and second-grade experience. Fourth, as in any effective literacy classroom, a number of activities usually occur concurrently. Fifth, and most importantly, the circle represents a perspective, not a prescription.

As one examines the suggested components presented in the circle of instruction, it is appropriate to ask by what means and to what extent any one component contributes to literacy development. In Figure 14, I list how selected components or elements contribute to the learning-to-read process.

Each component makes significant contributions to the learning to read process. Moreover, there is redundancy built into the system. For example, several instructional strategies address the learning and application of phonics. Phonics is learned through focused instruction, but phonics is also learned and significantly reinforced through writing with invented spellings and through extensive reading experiences with predictable text, experience charts, and repeated readings. Several of the components address fluency, and several address comprehension (i.e., the constructing of meaning from text). Removing one or more of these instructional components in order to spend time on one or even two or three components may have deleterious effects on the learning-to-read process.

The Role of Phonics

The phonics component of a balanced literacy curriculum is the most controversial and deserves to be addressed in greater depth. This is not to suggest, however, that the phonics component is any more important than the other elements in a balanced literacy curriculum. Three questions guide my discussion of the role of phonics in learning to read: (a) What kind of phonics? (b) How much phonics? and (c) When should phonics be taught?

There are three questions to ask when discussing the role of phonics in the learning-to-read process: What kind of phonics? How much phonics? and When should phonics be taught?

What Kind of Phonics?

In the simplest terms, there are two primary approaches to phonics instruction: *analytic* and *synthetic*. Analytic phonics involves analyzing common elements with words—*fish*, *fox*, and *fan* begin alike with the letter *f*; *bake*, *cake*, and *rake* all rhyme. The words *ball* and *well* end with the same two letters. In this approach, sounds are studied primarily in the context of words. However, they are taught directly and explicitly. In a synthetic approach to phonics instruction, students are taught individual letter sounds—b has a *buh* sound, a an *ah* sound, and t a *tuh* sound. One then blends or synthesizes these sounds together—bah-ah-tuh, /b/a/t/, bat.

More recently, in the mid-1980s, the two approaches were renamed. Synthetic phonics is now referred to as explicit phonics, and analytic phonics is referred to as implicit phonics. The new labels may be unfortunate, for one can teach analytic phonics just as explicitly as one can teach synthetic phonics. It is difficult to ascertain whether the explicit terminology refers to the "isolation of sounds" or to a method of teaching, or both. Somehow, in this renewed focus on phonics issues, the debate about the kind or type of phonics instruction to be used in classrooms has not received the attention it warrants.

How Much Phonics Should Be Taught?

In my work with Stauffer on one of the first-grade studies commissioned by the United States Office of Education in the 1960s, we recommended that an average of twenty to twenty-five minutes a day be devoted to phonics, word study, or word recognition instruction in first- and second-grade classrooms (Stauffer, 1969; Stauffer & Hammond, 1969). Sometimes phonics was taught in a focused, direct manner;

at other times, phonics was taught in the context of other literacy activities. Interestingly, instruction began with a heavy concentration of auditory discrimination activities, which are the basis of phonemic awareness in the 1990s. However, we did not find the blending or segmentation activities that are so popular today to be a necessary component. In those early days, we were mindful that teachers not spend so much time on phonics and word recognition activities that other crucial components of the curriculum would be minimized or eliminated. The achievement results spoke for themselves as reported in the study (Stauffer & Hammond, 1969). Thirty years later there seems to be no persuasive evidence that phonics instruction, important though it is, should be the dominating instructional activity in a balanced curriculum.

When Should Phonics Be Taught?

Part of the debate about when phonics should be taught is whether teachers should begin with phonemic awareness prior to other experiences or engagement with literacy instruction. In the award winning Ayres (1993) study, kindergarten students who had language experiences and exposure to predictable books and Big Books first, and were then instructed in phonemic awareness, were more successful in literacy development than students who began with intensive phonemic awareness training. Based on this research, we can conclude that phonemic awareness and phonics are best taught in the context of, or concurrently with, other language and literacy experiences. The Ayres (1993) study, conducted in Michigan classrooms, makes a strong case for a balanced literacy curriculum.

In brief, phonics as an either/or proposition is far too simplistic. The type of phonics used, the amount of instructional time devoted to phonics instruction, and the timing of that instruction are critical issues that must be addressed.

Concluding Comment

The issue of how best to teach young children to read and write has been with us for more than a century. As we move into the twenty-first century, educators—both researchers and practitioners—must establish a common ground on this issue. No side or position should co-opt the "we are the scientists" mantra, nor should any side or position claim they have a monopoly on the humanist "we care more about children" perspective. Such posturing is counterproductive. There is room for healthy and civil debate, and most importantly, careful attention to anyone who can make a contribution.

This paper stresses a balanced curriculum for all students. My plea is that balance is particularly essential to the students who are our greatest challenges. These are the very students, the at-risk students, who need a multidimensional, interactive, and redundant literacy curriculum. These students cannot be relegated to a narrow one-dimensional approach, whatever that approach might be.

Clearly this is a confusing and contentious time as we enter the new millennium, even for those of us who have devoted most or all of our careers to literacy issues. Imagine the confusion of many school leaders and classroom teachers who don't have the luxury of focusing every working hour on literacy issues. Moreover, when the public at large sees divisiveness within our profession, our credibility is questioned.

Too often we have seen the pendulum swing from one extreme to the other in literacy programs. The

No side or position should co-opt the "we are the scientists" mantra, nor should any side or position claim that they have a monopoly on the humanist "we care more about children" perspective.

Balance is particularly essential to the students who are our greatest challenges. These are the very students, the at-risk students, who need a multidimensional, interactive, and redundant literacy curriculum.

pendulum has swung from an emphasis on excessive skills and drills to a view that reading is simply a case of immersing students into a literacy environment— from part learning to whole learning and back again. These continuing debates on early literacy and the role of phonics have distracted our profession from other critical literacy issues. For example, we need to focus on the nature of critical reading and reading comprehension as it relates to intermediate, middle, and secondary students. We need to consider the role and nature of literacy in a technological society, and the meaning of being a highly literate adult. We need to concentrate on the role of reading and writing in the self-actualization of children and adults, as well as the role of literacy in helping societies to remain free and democratic. This is only a partial list of the issues that require our professional attention.

That is why this article and the others in this monograph call for a balanced perspective. We feel balance is essential to providing the correct mix of educational experiences that will maximize learning and ensure that every child in the next millennium will be a thoughtful, critical, constructive, fluent, strategic, motivated, lifelong reader and writer.

References

Adams, M. J. (1990a). *Beginning to read: Thinking and learning about print.* Cambridge, MA: MIT Press.

Adams, M. J. (1990b). *Beginning to read: Thinking and learning about print—a summary.* Prepared by S. A. Stahl, J. Osborn, & F. Lehr. Urbana-Champaign, IL: Center for the Study of Reading.

Anderson, R. C., Hiebert, E. H., Scott, J. A., & Wilkinson, I. A. (1985). *Becoming a nation of readers: The report of the commission on reading.* Washington, DC: The National Institute of Education.

Ayres, L. (1993). The efficacy of three training conditions on phonological awareness of kindergarten children and the longitudinal effect of each on later reading acquisition. Unpublished doctoral dissertation, Oakland University.

Barone, D. (Ed.) (1997). *Reading Research Quarterly, 32.* Newark, DE: International Reading Association.

Chall, J. S. (1967). *Learning to read: The great debate.* New York: McGraw-Hill.

Flesch, R. (1955). *Why Johnny can't read.* New York: Harper and Row.

Goodman, K. (1992). Whole language research: Foundations and development. In J. Samuels & A. Farstrup (Eds.), *What research has to say about reading instruction,* (2nd ed.) (pp. 46–49). Newark, DE: International Reading Association.

Gough, P., Alford, J. A., & Holley-Wilcox, P. (1981). Words and contexts. In O. S. Tzeng & H. Singer (Eds.), *Perception of print: Reading research in experimental psychology* (pp. 85–102). Hillsdale, NJ: Erlbaum.

Graves, D. (1983). *Writing teachers and children at work.* Portsmouth, NH: Heinemann.

Heilman, A. (1993). *Phonics in proper perspective.* Columbus, OH: Merrill.

Holdaway, D. (1979). *The foundations of literacy.* Gotsford, New South Wales: Ashton Scholastic.

LaBerge, D., & Samuels, J. (1974). Toward a theory of automatic information processing in reading. *Cognitive Psychology, 6,* 293–323.

Levine, A. (1994). The great debate revisited. *Atlantic Monthly, 274* (6), 38–44.

Lyon, R. C. (1998). Why reading is not a natural act. *Educational Leadership, 15*, 14–18.

Martin, B. (1963). *Brown bear, brown bear, what do you see?* New York: Holt, Rinehart & Winston.

Perfetti, C., & Zhang, S. (1996). What it means to learn to read. In M. Graves, P. van den Broek, & B. Taylor (Eds.), *The first R: Every child's right to read* (pp. 36–61). New York: Teachers College Press.

Routman, R. (1988). *Transitions.* Portsmouth, NH: Heinemann.

Samuels, S. J. (1979). The method of repeated readings. *The Reading Teacher, 32*, 403–408.

Stauffer, R. G. (1970). *The language experience approach to the teaching of reading.* New York: Harper & Row.

Stauffer, R. G., & Hammond, W. D. (1969). Effectiveness of a language arts and basic reader approach to first grade instruction: Extended into third grade. *Reading Research Quarterly, 4*, 468–499.

Texas Education Agency. (1988). *Texas reading proclamation.* Austin, TX: Author.

Texas Education Agency. (1997). *Texas reading initiative.* Austin, TX: Author.

Weaver, C. (1994). *Reading process and practice.* Portsmouth, NH: Heinemann.

Wells, G. (1986). *The meaning makers.* Portsmouth, NH: Heinemann.